1001 ESSENTIAL SENTENCES
FOR ELEMENTARY ENGLISH LEARNERS

CEDU 쎄듀는 A **C**omprehensive **E**nglish e**DU**cation(종합적 영어교육)의 약자입니다.

펴낸이	김기훈 · 김진희
펴낸곳	(주)쎄듀 / 서울시 강남구 논현로 305 (역삼동)
발행일	2016년 11월 28일 초판 1쇄
내용문의	www.cedubook.com
구입문의	콘텐츠 마케팅 사업본부
	Tel. 02-6241-2007
	Fax. 02-2058-0209
등록번호	제 22-2472호
ISBN	978-89-6806-078-6

초 등 코 치

천일문
sentence

✦ ✦ ✦

3

저자

김기훈   現 ㈜ 쎄듀 대표이사
           現 메가스터디 영어영역 대표강사
           前 서울특별시 교육청 외국어 교육정책자문위원회 위원
    저서 천일문 / 천일문 Training Book / 천일문 GRAMMAR / 초등코치 천일문
           어법끝 / 어휘끝 / 첫단추 / 쎈쓰업 / 파워업 / 빈칸백서 / 오답백서
           쎄듀 본영어 / 문법의 골든룰 101 / ALL씀 서술형 / 수능실감
           거침없이 Writing / Grammar Q / Reading Q / Listening Q
           왓츠 그래머 / 왓츠 리딩 / 패턴으로 말하는 초등 필수 영단어 등

쎄듀 영어교육연구센터
쎄듀 영어교육센터는 영어 콘텐츠에 대한 전문지식과 경험을 바탕으로
최고의 교육 콘텐츠를 만들고자 최선의 노력을 다하는 전문가 집단입니다.
인지영 책임연구원 · **장혜승** 선임연구원

검토위원

성윤선   現 Charles G. Emery Elementary School 교사
    약력 하버드대학교 교육대학원 Language and Literacy 석사
           이화여자대학교 교육공학, 영어교육 복수 전공
           가톨릭대학교 교수학습센터 연구원
           이화여자대학교 교수학습개발원 연구원
           한국교육개발원 연구원

마케팅	콘텐츠 마케팅 사업본부
영업	문병구
제작	정승호
인디자인 편집	올댓에디팅
표지 디자인	윤혜영
내지 디자인	에피그램
영문교열	Eric Scheusner

Foreword

〈초등코치 천일문 SENTENCE〉 시리즈를 펴내며

초등 영어, 무엇을 어떻게 시작해야 할까요?

자녀에게 영어 공부를 시키는 목적은 여러 가지일 것입니다. '우리 아이가 원어민처럼 영어를 잘했으면 좋겠다', '생활하는 데 영어가 걸림돌이 되지 않으면 좋겠다'라는 바람에서, 또는 중학교 내신이나 대학 입시를 위해 영어 공부를 시키기도 하지요.

영어를 공부하는 목표가 무엇이 되든, 영어의 기초가 잡혀 있지 않으면 새로운 것을 배우는 데 시간과 노력이 더 많이 들 수밖에 없습니다. 그리고 영어는 아이가 공부해야 하는 단 하나의 과목이 아니기에, 영어 공부에 비교적 많은 시간을 투자할 수 있는 초등학생 시기가 매우 중요하지요.

〈초등코치 천일문 SENTENCE〉 시리즈는 기초를 세우기에 가장 적절한 초등학생 시기에 **1,001개 통문장 암기로 영어의 기초를 완성**할 수 있도록 기획되었습니다. 1,001개 문장은 꼭 알아야 할 패턴 112개와 실생활에 유용한 표현들로 구성되었습니다.

| 문장과 덩어리 표현(chunk)이 학습의 주가 됩니다.

영어를 학습할 때는 문장(full sentence)과 덩어리 표현(chunk) 학습법이 더욱 효과적입니다. 〈초등코치 천일문 SENTENCE〉는 우리말 설명을 최소화하고 문장 자체에 집중할 수 있도록 구성했습니다. 책에 수록된 모든 문장과 표현, 대화는 現 미국 공립 초등학교 선생님의 검토를 받아 완성되었습니다.

| 문장 암기를 쉽게 할 수 있도록 설계했습니다.

문장과 표현이 자연스럽게 7번 반복되어 책을 따라 하다 보면 자동으로 1,001개 문장을 암기할 수 있습니다. 그리고 이해와 기억을 돕기 위해 재미있는 그림으로 새로운 표현들과 상황을 제시했습니다. 또한, 대부분 문장의 주어를 '나(I)'로 하여 아이들이 실생활에서도 자주 말하고 쓸 수 있도록 했습니다.

1,001개 통문장 암기로 탄탄한 기초가 세워지면, 내신, 수능, 말하기·듣기 등 앞으로의 모든 영어 학습에 대한 불안감이 해소될 것입니다. 〈초등코치 천일문 SENTENCE〉 시리즈와의 만남을 통해 영어 학습이 더욱더 쉬워지고 즐거워지는 경험을 꼭 할 수 있기를 희망합니다.

저 자

추천의 글

외국어 학습은 수년의 시간이 수반되는 장거리 경주입니다. 따라서, 잘못된 방식으로 학습을 시작해 외국어 학습의 즐거움을 초반에 잃어버리면, 끝까지 지속하지 못하고 중도에 포기하게 됩니다. 쎄듀의 초등코치 천일문은 대한민국의 초등 영어 학습자들이 효과적이고 효율적으로 영어학습의 경주를 시작할 수 있도록 여러분의 걸음을 친절하고 꼼꼼하게 안내해 줍니다.

효과적인 초등 영어 학습을 약속합니다.

영어 학습 과정에서 단어를 하나하나 익히는 것도 물론 중요하지만, 덩어리(chunk) 또는 패턴으로 다양한 영어 표현을 익히면 영어를 보다 유창하게 구사하고, 빠른 속도로 이해할 수 있습니다. 쎄듀의 초등코치 천일문은 일상 생활에서 가장 빈번히 사용되는 112개의 문장 패턴을 담았습니다.

또한, 각 문장 패턴당 8~9개의 훈련 문장들과 함께 4개의 짧은 대화가 수록되어 해당 패턴을 실제로 어떻게 사용할 수 있는지 보여줍니다. 이렇게 다양한 예문과 구체적인 대화 상황을 제시함으로써 쎄듀 초등코치 천일문은 언어 학습에 필수적인 패턴을 활용한 반복 학습을 이루어 갑니다.

112개의 필수 영어 문장 패턴과 이를 활용한 1,001개의 예문 학습, 그리고 구석구석 꼼꼼하게 안내된 어휘 학습까지. 쎄듀의 초등코치 천일문은 영어 학습을 시작하는 학생들이 탄탄한 영어의 기초를 다질 수 있는 효과적인 학습방법을 제시합니다.

효율적인 초등 영어 학습을 약속합니다.

애써 영어 공부를 했는데, 실제 영어를 사용하는 현장에서 활용할 수 없다면 어떻게 해야 할까요? 기존의 학습 내용을 지우고, 출발점으로 돌아가 다시 시작해야 합니다. 장거리를 달려야 하는데 다시 시작이라니 지칠 수밖에 없습니다.

쎄듀의 초등코치 천일문은 한 문장 한 문장, 대화 하나하나를 미국 초등학생들이 실제로 사용하는지 철저히 고려하여 엄선된 내용을 채택하였습니다. 초등학생들의 관심 주제를 바탕으로 문장과 대화들이 작성되어 학습자 모두 내용을 친숙하게 느낄 수 있습니다.

친숙한 대화 소재를 바탕으로 한 실제적인 영어 예문 학습을 통해, 본 교재를 이용한 학생들은 잘못된 공부로 인한 소진 없이 효율적으로 영어의 기본기를 다질 수 있습니다.

LA에서, 성윤선

Series

1권 Track 01~24 001-212	2권 Track 25~48 213-428	3권 Track 49~70 429-624	4권 Track 71~91 625-813	5권 Track 92~112 814-1001
This is ~.	I can ~.	I'm going to ~.	I started -ing.	Give me ~.
That's ~.	I can't ~.	He[She]'s going to ~.	I began to ~.	He[She] gave me ~.
I am a/an ~.	You can ~.	Are you going to ~?	Stop -ing.	I'll show you ~.
I am ~.	Can I ~?	I was about to ~.	I[We] kept -ing.	I'll tell you ~.
I'm not ~.	Can you ~?	I'm -ing.	I want to ~.	It makes me ~.
You are ~.	I[You] should ~.	He[She]'s -ing.	I don't want to ~.	He[She, It] made me ~.
He[She] is ~.	You must ~.	Are you -ing?	I wanted to ~.	Let me ~.
He[She] is in ~.	I[You] might ~.	I was -ing.	I like to ~.	Help me ~.
It is ~.	I have to ~.	What's ~?	I need to ~.	I want you to ~.
Are you ~?	You have to ~.	What do you ~?	I tried to ~.	I saw him[her] -ing.
It's ~.	You don't have to ~.	What are you -ing?	I'm supposed to ~.	I heard him[her] -ing.
There is ~.	I had to ~.	Who is ~?	It's time to ~.	I think (that) ~.
There are ~.	I used to ~.	Why do you ~?	Do you know how to ~?	I don't think (that) ~.
Is[Are] there any ~?	I was ~.	Why don't we ~?	I don't know what to ~.	I thought (that) ~.
There's no ~.	He[She] was ~.	Where is ~?	He[She] seems to ~.	I know (that) ~.
I have ~.	I went to ~.	Where did you ~?	You look ~.	I knew (that) ~.
He[She] has ~.	I put it ~.	How do you ~?	I feel ~.	I don't know what ~.
I want ~.	I didn't ~.	When are you going to ~?	I got ~.	I guess (that) ~.
I like ~.	Did you ~?	What a[an]~!	I'm getting ~.	I hope (that) ~.
I hate ~.	I[We] will ~.	Do[Be] ~.	He[She] seems ~.	I'm sure (that) ~.
I need ~.	He[She] will ~.	Don't ~.	It looks like ~.	That's why ~.
I don't ~.	I won't ~.	Let's ~.		
Do you ~?	I'll be able to ~.			
Does he[she] ~?	Will you ~?			

Preview

Step 1

대표 문장과 패턴을 확인합니다.
미국 도서관 협회 추천 영어 동화책을 분석하여 가장 많이 쓰이는 패턴
112가지를 쉽고 간략한 설명과 함께 여러 예문으로 제시했습니다.

QR코드

휴대폰을 통해 QR 코드를 인식하면, 본문의 모든
문장, 단어 및 청크, 대화의 MP3 파일이 재생됩니다.

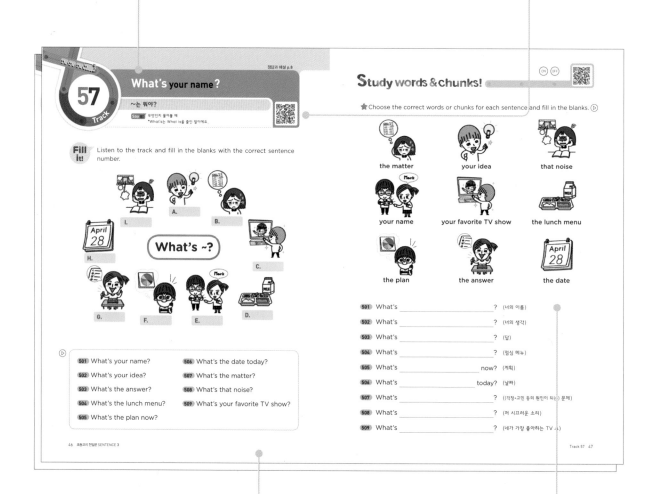

Step 2

미국 현지 초등학생 원어민 성우들이 읽는 문장들을
듣고 그림과 연결합니다.
귀로 듣고 눈으로 보면서 직접 패턴과 청크들을 연결합니다. 보기와
듣기까지 동시에 함으로써 학습 내용을 오래 기억할 수 있습니다.

Step 3

단어와 청크를 집중적으로 연습합니다.
단어와 청크 뜻에 맞는 그림을 연결해 보면서
문장을 완성합니다. 실생활에서 자주 쓸 수 있는
유용한 표현들을 익힐 수 있습니다.

Step 4

각 그림 상황에 알맞은 문장을 완성합니다.
앞에서 배운 패턴과 청크를 사용하여 완전한 문장을 써 봅니다. 재미있는 그림을 통해 문장이 실제로 사용되는 상황을 알 수 있습니다.

Step 5

각 대화 상황에 알맞은 문장을 넣어 봅니다.
학습한 문장이 실제로 어떤 대화 상황에서 쓰일 수 있는지 확실하게 알 수 있습니다.

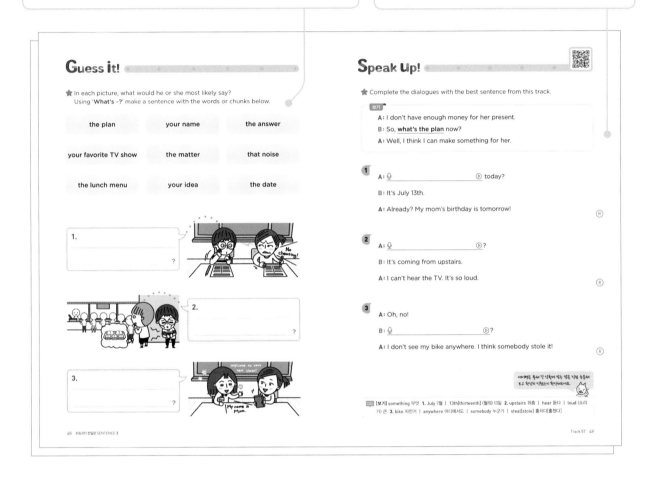

Step 6

워크북으로 단어 및 청크, 문장을 마스터합니다.

Step 7

무료 부가서비스 자료로 완벽하게 복습합니다.

1. 어휘리스트 2. 어휘테스트 3. 본문 해석 연습지
4. 본문 말하기·영작 연습지 5. MP3 파일
* 모든 자료는 www.cedubook.com에서 다운로드 가능합니다.

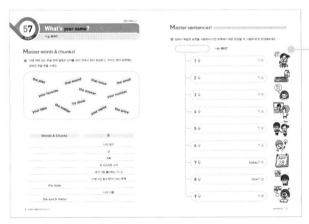

MP3 활용하기

〈초등코치 천일문 SENTENCE〉 부가서비스 자료에는 본문의 모든 문장, 단어 및 청크, 대화의 MP3 파일이 들어 있습니다.

• 미국 현지 초등학생 원어민 성우의 생생하고 정확한 발음과 억양을 확인할 수 있습니다.

• 문장은 2회씩 녹음되어 있습니다.

Strong Points

1 20일 또는 16일 완성

〈초등코치 천일문 SENTENCE〉 시리즈는 한 권을 20일 또는 16일 동안 학습할 수 있도록 구성되어 있습니다. 아이의 상황에 맞게 계획표를 선택하여 학습할 수 있습니다.

2 복잡한 문법 설명 없이도 가능한 학습

어렵고 복잡한 문법 용어를 설명할 필요가 없습니다. 패턴과 문장 자체의 의미를 받아들이는 데 집중하도록 구성되어 부담 없이 학습해 나갈 수 있습니다.

3 문장이 자연스럽게 외워지는 자동 암기 시스템

각 트랙에는 8~9개의 문장이 수록되어 있습니다. 본책과 워크북에는 이러한 문장들과 문장 속 표현들이 7번이나 자연스럽게 반복되는 효과가 있어서 책을 따라 하다 보면 자동적으로 암기가 가능합니다.

★ MP3 파일을 반복해서 들으면 암기에 더욱 효과적입니다.
책에 실린 모든 문장은 초등학생 원어민 성우 Arthur와 Claire가 미국 현지에서 녹음했습니다.

✏ 세이펜으로 더 쉽게, 더 자주 반복해서 들을 수 있습니다.
또한, Study words & chunks의 게임 기능을 통해 더욱 재미있게 암기할 수 있습니다.

4 이해와 기억을 돕는 1,337개의 그림

그림과 상황을 통해 문장의 의미를 직관적으로 이해할 수 있도록 1,001개의 표현을 묘사한 그림과 336개의 대화 상황을 나타내는 그림을 실었습니다.

my mistake

⑤ 또래 원어민 친구와 나눠보는 대화

각 트랙의 마지막 페이지에는 학습한 문장을 채워볼 수 있는 dialogue 4개가 실려 있습니다. 이 대화는 모두 뉴욕에 거주하는 초등학생 원어민 성우 Eden과 Kara가 미국 현지에서 녹음한 것으로, A와 B 중 골라서 role playing을 할 수 있습니다. 꾸준히 연습하다 보면, 실제로 원어민 친구를 만나도 당황하지 않고 자연스럽게 대화할 수 있습니다.

세이펜의 Role-Play 기능을 활용하여 더욱 생생한 대화를 경험해 볼 수 있습니다.
세이펜으로 각 dialogue의 빈칸을 포함한 문장 전체를 녹음한 후 Role-Play 버튼 Ⓡ에 대면,
녹음한 문장이 원어민의 대화와 함께 자연스럽게 재생됩니다.

⑥ 다양한 부가 학습 자료로 완벽 복습

1,001개의 문장을 다양한 부가 학습 자료로 완벽하게 복습할 수 있습니다. 테스트 자료로도 유용하게 활용하실 수 있습니다.
(www.cedubook.com에서 무료로 다운로드 가능합니다.)

어휘리스트 & 어휘테스트
본문에 실린 모든 어휘를 학습할 수 있습니다. 어휘리스트로 학습한 후에는 어휘테스트로 어휘 실력을 점검해볼 수 있습니다.

본문 해석 연습지
1,001개 문장의 해석을 써보며 의미를 복습할 수 있습니다.

본문 말하기·영작 연습지
우리말 해석을 보고 영어로 바꿔 말하거나 써볼 수 있습니다.
말하기·영작 연습지는 '우리말 뜻을 보고 빈칸 채우기 ▶ 순서대로 어휘 배열하기 ▶ 뜻을 보며 영작하기'의 순서로 구성되어 있습니다.

9

Contents 📖

책속책 WORKBOOK | 정답과 해설

Study Plan

★ 20일 완성!

	Track	공부한 날짜	
1일차	Track 49, 워크북/Track 50, 워크북	월	일
2일차	Track 51, 워크북/Track 52, 워크북	월	일
3일차	Track 53, 워크북/Track 54, 워크북	월	일
4일차	Track 55, 워크북/Track 56, 워크북	월	일
5일차	Track 49~50 Review	월	일
6일차	Track 51~52 Review	월	일
7일차	Track 53~54 Review	월	일
8일차	Track 55~56 Review	월	일
9일차	Track 57, 워크북/Track 58, 워크북	월	일
10일차	Track 59, 워크북/Track 60, 워크북	월	일
11일차	Track 61, 워크북/Track 62, 워크북	월	일
12일차	Track 63, 워크북/Track 64, 워크북	월	일
13일차	Track 57~59 Review	월	일
14일차	Track 60~62 Review	월	일
15일차	Track 63~64 Review	월	일
16일차	Track 65, 워크북/Track 66, 워크북	월	일
17일차	Track 67, 워크북/Track 68, 워크북	월	일
18일차	Track 69, 워크북/Track 70, 워크북	월	일
19일차	Track 65~67 Review	월	일
20일차	Track 68~70 Review	월	일

★ 16일 완성!

	Track	공부한 날짜	
1일차	Track 49~51, 워크북	월	일
2일차	Track 49~51 Review	월	일
3일차	Track 52~54, 워크북	월	일
4일차	Track 52~54 Review	월	일
5일차	Track 55~57, 워크북	월	일
6일차	Track 55~57 Review	월	일
7일차	Track 58~60, 워크북	월	일
8일차	Track 58~60 Review	월	일
9일차	Track 61~63, 워크북	월	일
10일차	Track 61~63 Review	월	일
11일차	Track 64~65, 워크북	월	일
12일차	Track 64~65 Review	월	일
13일차	Track 66~67, 워크북	월	일
14일차	Track 66~67 Review	월	일
15일차	Track 68~70, 워크북	월	일
16일차	Track 68~70 Review	월	일

Let's Start!

49 Track

I'm going to play outside.

나는 ~할 거야.

Say It! 내가 앞으로 할 일에 대해 말할 때

Fill it! Listen to the track and fill in the blanks with the correct sentence number.

I. A. B.

H. **I'm going to ~.** C.

G. F. E. D.

429 I'm going to play outside.

430 I'm going to meet my friends.

431 I'm going to study harder.

432 I'm going to visit my grandparents.

433 I'm going to take a shower.

434 I'm going to sit by the window.

435 I'm going to eat out with my family.

436 I'm going to learn to swim.

437 I'm going to be in fourth grade next year.

Study words & chunks!

⭐ Choose the correct words or chunks for each sentence and fill in the blanks. ▷

visit my grandparents

sit by the window

meet my friends

play outside

be in fourth grade

eat out with my family

learn to swim

study harder

take a shower

429 I'm going to _____ . (밖에서 놀다)

430 I'm going to _____ . (내 친구들을 만나다)

431 I'm going to _____ . (더 열심히 공부하다)

432 I'm going to _____ . (나의 할머니, 할아버지를 방문하다)

433 I'm going to _____ . (샤워하다)

434 I'm going to _____ . (창가에 앉다)

435 I'm going to _____ . (나의 가족과 외식하다)

436 I'm going to _____ . (수영하는 것을 배우다)

437 I'm going to _____ next year. (4학년이 되다)

Guess it!

⭐ In each picture, what would he or she most likely say?
   Using '**I'm going to ~.**' make a sentence with the words or chunks below.

meet my friends	be in fourth grade	take a shower
eat out with my family	visit my grandparents	play outside
study harder	sit by the window	learn to swim

1.

_____

_____ .

2.

_____

_____ .

3.

_____

_____ .

Speak Up!

⭐ Complete the dialogues with the best sentence from this track.

> **보기**
>
> **A:** I studied hard, but my grade went down. I'm sad.
>
> **B:** Cheer up. You will do better next time.   *Cheer up. 힘내.
>
> **A:** Thanks. **I'm going to study harder**.

1

A: Do you have any plans today?

B: Yes. 🎤 _____ ▷.

A: That's great. Where will you go?

Ⓡ

2

A: What do you want to do during the vacation?

B: 🎤 _____ ▷. I want to swim well.

Ⓡ

3

A: 🎤 _____ ▷.

B: Okay. But why?

A: I get carsick. I'll feel better by the window.

Ⓡ

세이펜을 통해 각 상황에 맞는 말을 직접 녹음해
보고 확실히 익혔는지 확인해보세요.

📖 **[보기]** grade 성적 | go[went] down 내려가다[내려갔다] | do better 더 잘하다 | next time 다음번 **2.** want to ~하고 싶다 | vacation 방학 **3.** get carsick 차멀미하다

17

50
Track

He's going to be fine.

그[그녀]는 ~할 거야.

Say it! 다른 사람이 앞으로 할 일에 대해 말할 때
*He's, She's는 각각 He is, She is를 줄인 말이에요.

Fill it! Listen to the track and fill in the blanks with the correct sentence number.

I.

A.

B.

H.

He[She]'s going to ~.

C.

G.

F.

E.

D.

438 He's going to be fine.

439 He's going to be there.

440 She's going to be late.

441 She's going to call me.

442 He's going to help me.

443 She's going to love it.

444 He's going to make it.

445 She's going to be surprised.

446 She's going to be the class president.

Study words & chunks!

⭐ Choose the correct words or chunks for each sentence and fill in the blanks. ▷

be surprised

be late

love it

make it

be the class president

be fine

help me

be there

call me

438	He's going to _____.	(괜찮다)
439	He's going to _____.	(그곳에 있다)
440	She's going to _____.	(늦다)
441	She's going to _____.	(나에게 전화하다)
442	He's going to _____.	(나를 도와주다)
443	She's going to _____.	(그것을 정말 좋아하다)
444	He's going to _____.	(해내다)
445	She's going to _____.	(놀라다)
446	She's going to _____.	(반장이 되다)

Guess it!

⭐ In each picture, what would he or she most likely say?
Using '**He[She]'s going to ~.**' make a sentence with the words or chunks below.

call me	be surprised	help me
be the class president	make it	be there
be fine	be late	love it

1. _____
   _____ .

2. _____
   _____ .

3. _____
   _____ .

Speak Up!

⭐ Complete the dialogues with the best sentence from this track.

> **보기**
>
> **A:** I can finish it on time.
>
> **B:** Are you sure? It's due tomorrow.
>
> **A:** My brother is home right now. **He's going to help me**.

1

A: Where is she?

B: She will come soon. 🎤 _____ ▷.

A: Oh! Your cell phone is ringing. It must be her.

Ⓡ

2

A: Don't worry. 🎤 _____ ▷.

B: But he didn't look fine.

A: He is resting in the nurse's office. He will get better.

Ⓡ

3

A: Where is Sara?

B: She messaged me. 🎤 _____ ▷.

A: Okay. Let's wait inside.

Ⓡ

세이펜을 통해 각 상황에 맞는 말을 직접 녹음해
보고 확실히 익혔는지 확인해보세요.

📖 **[보기]** on time 제시간에 | sure 확실한 | due (언제) ~하기로 되어 있는 **1.** soon 곧 | cell phone 휴대폰 | ring (전화가) 울리다 | must ~임이 틀림없다 **2.** rest 쉬다 | nurse's office 보건실 | get better 나아지다, 좋아지다 **3.** Sara 사라(여자 이름) | message[messaged] 메시지를 보내다[보냈다]

51 Track

Are you going to say yes?

너는 ~할 거야?

Say It! 상대방에게 앞으로 할 일에 대해 물어볼 때

Fill it! Listen to the track and fill in the blanks with the correct sentence number.

I.   A.   B.   C.

Are you going to ~?

H.   G.   F.   E.   D.

447 Are you going to sit here?

448 Are you going to eat that?

449 Are you going to say yes?

450 Are you going to buy something?

451 Are you going to tell your mom?

452 Are you going to take the bus?

453 Are you going to come with us?

454 Are you going to be mad at me?

455 Are you going to come to my birthday party?

Study words & chunks!

⭐ Choose the correct words or chunks for each sentence and fill in the blanks. ▶

be mad at me

eat that

take the bus

buy something

come with us

sit here

say yes

come to my birthday party

tell your mom

447 Are you going to _____? (여기에 앉다)

448 Are you going to _____? (그것을 먹다)

449 Are you going to _____? (그렇다고 말하다)

450 Are you going to _____? (무언가를 사다)

451 Are you going to _____? (너의 엄마께 말씀드리다)

452 Are you going to _____? (버스를 타다)

453 Are you going to _____? (우리와 함께 가다)

454 Are you going to _____? (나에게 화가 나다)

455 Are you going to _____? (내 생일 파티에 오다)

Guess it!

⭐ In each picture, what would he or she most likely say?
Using '**Are you going to ~?**' make a sentence with the words or chunks below.

say yes	buy something	eat that
come with us	be mad at me	sit here
come to my birthday party	tell your mom	take the bus

1.

_____
_____ ?

2.

_____
_____ ?

3.

_____
_____ ?

Speak Up!

⭐ Complete the dialogues with the best sentence from this track.

> **보기**
>
> **A:** Dan said he wants to join our team.
>
> **B: Are you going to say yes**?
>
> **A:** I'm not sure. Let's talk about it.

1

A: 🎤 _____ ▷ ?

B: No, I am full. You can have it.

Ⓡ

2

A: I think I lost my wallet.

B: 🎤 _____ ▷ ?

A: I already did. She is on the way here now.

Ⓡ

3

A: What did you say to her? Tell me!

B: 🎤 _____ ▷ ?

A: Ha! That depends.   *That depends. 상황에 따라 다르겠지.

Ⓡ

> 세이펜을 통해 각 상황에 맞는 말을 직접 녹음해
> 보고 확실히 익혔는지 확인해보세요.

📖 **[보기]** Dan 댄(남자 이름) | say[said] 말하다[말했다] | want to ~하고 싶다 | let's ~하자 **1.** have 먹다
2. lose[lost] 잃어버리다[잃어버렸다] | wallet 지갑 | on the way here 여기로 오는 중에

52 Track

I was about to tell you.

나는 막 ~하려던 참이었어.

Say It! 내가 방금 하려고 했던 일을 말할 때

Fill it! Listen to the track and fill in the blanks with the correct sentence number.

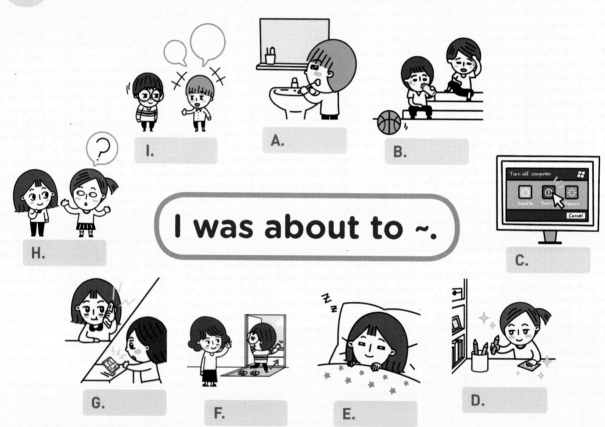

I.

A.

B.

I was about to ~.

H.

C.

G.

F.

E.

D.

456 I was about to call you.

457 I was about to tell you.

458 I was about to go out.

459 I was about to clean my desk.

460 I was about to brush my teeth.

461 I was about to fall asleep.

462 I was about to take a break.

463 I was about to ask you something.

464 I was about to turn the computer off.

Study words & chunks!

⭐ Choose the correct words or chunks for each sentence and fill in the blanks. ▷

tell you

take a break

ask you something

turn the computer off

fall asleep

brush my teeth

clean my desk

go out

call you

456 I was about to _____. (너에게 전화하다)

457 I was about to _____. (너에게 말하다)

458 I was about to _____. (나가다, 외출하다)

459 I was about to _____. (내 책상을 치우다)

460 I was about to _____. (양치질하다)

461 I was about to _____. (잠들다)

462 I was about to _____. (잠시 쉬다)

463 I was about to _____. (너에게 무언가를 물어보다)

464 I was about to _____. (컴퓨터를 끄다)

Guess it!

⭐ In each picture, what would he or she most likely say?
Using 'I was about to ~.' make a sentence with the words or chunks below.

tell you	go out	ask you something
turn the computer off	call you	fall asleep
brush my teeth	take a break	clean my desk

1.
_____
_____ .

2.
_____
_____ .

3.
_____
_____ .

Speak Up!

⭐ Complete the dialogues with the best sentence from this track.

보기

A: Why did you keep that a secret?

B: Sorry, but **I was about to tell you**. I just didn't have time to talk to you.

1

A: It's rainy now. But I don't have an umbrella.

B: You can share mine with me. 🎤 _____ ▷. ⓡ

2

A: Hey, what are you doing?

B: Oh, you came. 🎤 _____ ▷.

A: Really? I thought you were studying hard. ⓡ

3

A: Do you have to go now? 🎤 _____ ▷.

B: No, I am not in a hurry. What is it?

A: It's about this question. I just don't understand. ⓡ

> 세이펜을 통해 각 상황에 맞는 말을 직접 녹음해
> 보고 확실히 익혔는지 확인해보세요.

📖 **[보기]** secret 비밀 **1.** share 함께 쓰다 | mine 내 것 **2.** come[came] 오다[왔다] | think[thought] (~라고) 생각하다[생각했다] **3.** have to ~해야 한다 | in a hurry 바쁜, 서두르는

53

Track

I'm going to school.

나는 ~하고 있어.

Say It! 내가 지금 하고 있는 것을 말할 때

Fill it! Listen to the track and fill in the blanks with the correct sentence number.

I'm -ing.

I.

A.

B.

C.

D.

E.

F.

G.

H.

465 I'm having fun.

466 I'm eating dinner.

467 I'm going to school.

468 I'm listening to you.

469 I'm playing a game.

470 I'm sitting behind you.

471 I'm talking on the phone.

472 I'm thinking about something.

473 I'm looking for something.

Study words & chunks!

⭐ Choose the correct words or chunks for each sentence and fill in the blanks. ▷

playing a game

having fun

looking for something

going to school

talking on the phone

eating dinner

thinking about
something

listening to you

sitting behind you

465 I'm _____ . (재미있게 놀고 있는)

466 I'm _____ . (저녁을 먹고 있는)

467 I'm _____ . (학교에 가고 있는)

468 I'm _____ . (네 말을 듣고 있는)

469 I'm _____ . (게임을 하고 있는)

470 I'm _____ . (네 뒤에 앉아 있는)

471 I'm _____ . (전화 통화를 하고 있는)

472 I'm _____ . (무언가를 생각하고 있는)

473 I'm _____ . (무언가를 찾고 있는)

Guess it!

⭐ In each picture, what would he or she most likely say?
Using 'I'm -ing.' make a sentence with the words or chunks below.

having fun	going to school	listening to you
looking for something	playing a game	eating dinner
thinking about something	sitting behind you	talking on the phone

1. _____

   _____ .

2. _____

   _____ .

3. _____

   _____ .

Speak Up!

⭐ Complete the dialogues with the best sentence from this track.

> **보기**
>
> **A:** What are you doing?
>
> **B:** **I'm playing a game.**
>
> **A:** It looks fun. What is the name of it?

1

A: What are you doing?

B: 🎤 _____ ▷.

A: What do you need? I can help you.

Ⓡ

2

A: Yesterday, I went to ... Hey! I'm talking to you.

B: 🎤 _____ ▷. Go ahead.   *Go ahead. 계속해.

Ⓡ

3

A: Why are you so serious?

B: 🎤 _____ ▷.

A: About what? Can you tell me?

Ⓡ

세이펜을 통해 각 상황에 맞는 말을 직접 녹음해
보고 확실히 익혔는지 확인해보세요.

📖 **[보기]** look ~해 보이다 **3.** serious 심각한

54 Track

He's **eating** lunch.

그[그녀]는 ～하고 있어.

Say It! 다른 사람이 지금 하고 있는 일을 말할 때

Fill it! Listen to the track and fill in the blanks with the correct sentence number.

 I.

 A.

 B.

 H.

He[She]'s -ing.

 C.

 G.

 F.

 E.

 D.

474 He's eating lunch.

475 She's wearing a blue shirt.

476 He's making loud noises.

477 She's standing by the door.

478 He's sitting by the window.

479 She's looking in the mirror.

480 He's coming out of the classroom.

481 She's talking about her new class.

482 She's whispering to her friend.

Study words & chunks!

⭐ Choose the correct words or chunks for each sentence and fill in the blanks. ▷

looking in the mirror

standing by the door

making loud noises

whispering to her friend

talking about
her new class

sitting by the window

eating lunch

wearing a blue shirt

coming out of
the classroom

474 He's _____. (점심을 먹고 있는)

475 She's _____. (파란색 셔츠를 입고 있는)

476 He's _____. (시끄러운 소리를 내고 있는)

477 She's _____. (문 옆에 서 있는)

478 He's _____. (창가에 앉아 있는)

479 She's _____. (거울을 보고 있는)

480 He's _____. (교실 밖으로 나오고 있는)

481 She's _____. (그녀의 새로운 반에 대해 말하고 있는)

482 She's _____. (그녀의 친구에게 귓속말하고 있는)

Guess it!

⭐ In each picture, what would he or she most likely say?
Using 'He[She]'s -ing.' make a sentence with the words or chunks below.

wearing a blue shirt	looking in the mirror	whispering to her friend
eating lunch	making loud noises	standing by the door
sitting by the window	talking about her new class	coming out of the classroom

1.

2.

3.

Speak Up!

⭐ Complete the dialogues with the best sentence from this track.

> **보기**
>
> **A:** Where is he? I have to give this back to him.
>
> **B:** Look! **He's coming out of the classroom**.
>
> **A:** Oh, there he is. Thanks.
>
> *There he is. 그가 저기 있어.

1

A: 🎤 _____ ▷. What is he doing?

B: He's moving a desk and a chair outside.

A: It's really noisy.

Ⓡ

2

A: Let's go outside.

B: But we have to wait for Ted. 🎤 _____ ▷.

A: Still? The lunchtime will be over soon.

Ⓡ

3

A: Where is his seat? I can't see him.

B: 🎤 _____ ▷.

A: Oh, I found him.

Ⓡ

> 세이펜을 통해 각 상황에 맞는 말을 직접 녹음해
> 보고 확실히 익혔는지 확인해보세요.

📖 **[보기]** have to ~해야 한다 | give A back to B A를 B에게 돌려주다 **1.** move 옮기다 | outside 바깥으로, 밖에 | really 정말로 | noisy 시끄러운 **2.** Ted 테드(남자 이름) | still 아직도 | lunchtime 점심시간 | over 끝이 난 | soon 곧 **3.** seat 자리 | find[found] 찾다[찾았다]

55
Track

Are you going home?

너는 ~하고 있어?

Say It! 상대방이 지금 하고 있는 것을 물어볼 때

Fill it! Listen to the track and fill in the blanks with the correct sentence number.

I.

A.

B.

H.

Are you -ing?

C.

G.

F.

E.

D.

483 Are you going home?

484 Are you feeling okay?

485 Are you having fun?

486 Are you being honest?

487 Are you kidding me?

488 Are you coming or not?

489 Are you waiting for someone?

490 Are you studying for the test?

491 Are you looking for something?

Study words & chunks!

⭐ Choose the correct words or chunks for each sentence and fill in the blanks. ▷

kidding me

going home

looking for something

waiting for someone

feeling okay

studying for the test

coming or not

having fun

being honest

483 Are you _____ ?	(집에 가고 있는)
484 Are you _____ ?	(기분이 괜찮은)
485 Are you _____ ?	(재미있게 놀고 있는)
486 Are you _____ ?	((말이나 행동을) 솔직하게 하고 있는)
487 Are you _____ ?	(나에게 농담하고 있는)
488 Are you _____ ?	(오고 있는지 아닌지)
489 Are you _____ ?	(누군가를 기다리고 있는)
490 Are you _____ ?	(시험공부를 하고 있는)
491 Are you _____ ?	(무언가를 찾고 있는)

Guess it!

⭐ In each picture, what would he or she most likely say?
Using '**Are you –ing?**' make a sentence with the words or chunks below.

looking for something	waiting for someone	having fun
feeling okay	studying for the test	being honest
coming or not	kidding me	going home

1. _____
   _____ ?

2. _____
   _____ ?

3. _____
   _____ ?

Speak Up!

⭐ Complete the dialogues with the best sentence from this track.

> **보기**
>
> **A:** Hi. Where are you going?
>
> **B:** I'm going to the park. **Are you going home**?
>
> **A:** Yes. I'm on my way home from my Taekwondo lesson.

1

A: What are you doing here?

🎤 _____ ▷?

B: Yes. I'm supposed to meet my friend here.

Ⓡ

2

A: You look great in the picture.

B: 🎤 _____ ▷? I closed my eyes!

A: I think it looks cute.

Ⓡ

3

A: 🎤 _____ ▷?

B: Yes. I put my notebook in my bag, but I don't see it.

Ⓡ

세이펜을 통해 각 상황에 맞는 말을 직접 녹음해 보고 확실히 익혔는지 확인해보세요.

📖 **[보기]** on my way home (내가) 집으로 가는 중에 | Taekwondo 태권도 **1.** am[are, is] supposed to ~하기로 되어있다 **2.** look ~해 보이다 | close[closed] my eyes 내 눈을 감다[감았다] **3.** put[put] 넣다[넣었다] | notebook 공책

56
Track

I was **help**ing my mom.

나는 ~하고 있었어.

Say it! 과거에 내가 하고 있었던 일을 말할 때

Fill it! Listen to the track and fill in the blanks with the correct sentence number.

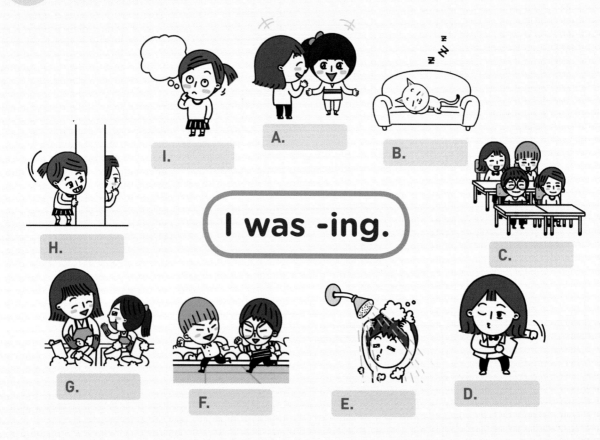

I.

A.

B.

H.

I was -ing.

C.

G.

F.

E.

D.

492 I was playing outside.

493 I was thinking about it.

494 I was helping my mom.

495 I was taking a shower.

496 I was looking for you.

497 I was talking to my friend.

498 I was sitting in a classroom.

499 I was sleeping on the couch.

500 I was getting ready to leave.

Study words & chunks!

⭐ Choose the correct words or chunks for each sentence and fill in the blanks. ▷

getting ready to leave

playing outside

sleeping on the couch

helping my mom

looking for you

taking a shower

sitting in a classroom

talking to my friend

thinking about it

492 I was _____. (밖에서 놀고 있는)

493 I was _____. (그것에 대해 생각하고 있는)

494 I was _____. (엄마를 도와드리고 있는)

495 I was _____. (샤워를 하고 있는)

496 I was _____. (너를 찾고 있는)

497 I was _____. (내 친구와 이야기하고 있는)

498 I was _____. (교실 안에 앉아 있는)

499 I was _____. (소파에서 자고 있는)

500 I was _____. (떠날 준비를 하고 있는)

Guess it!

⭐ In each picture, what would he or she most likely say?
Using 'I was –ing.' make a sentence with the words or chunks below.

taking a shower	sleeping on the couch	looking for you
sitting in a classroom	talking to my friend	helping my mom
playing outside	thinking about it	getting ready to leave

1.

2.

3.

Speak Up!

⭐ Complete the dialogues with the best sentence from this track.

> **보기**
>
> **A:** It suddenly rained a lot yesterday.
>
> **B:** Yes. **I was playing outside**. I got wet in the rain.

1

A: Why didn't you answer the phone?

B: I was in the bathroom. I sweated a lot, so 🎤 _____
_____ ▷. Ⓡ

2

A: I saw you in the supermarket yesterday.

B: Really? 🎤 _____ ▷. We had many
things to buy. Ⓡ

3

A: Where were you? 🎤 _____ ▷. Ⓡ

B: I went to the bathroom. Why?

세이펜을 통해 각 상황에 맞는 말을 직접 녹음해
보고 확실히 익혔는지 확인해보세요.

📖 **[보기]** suddenly 갑자기 ǀ a lot 많이 ǀ get[got] wet 물에 젖다[젖었다] **1.** answer the phone 전화를 받다 ǀ
sweat[sweated] 땀을 흘리다[흘렸다] **2.** see[saw] 보다[보았다] ǀ supermarket 슈퍼마켓 ǀ really 정말
3. go[went] to ~에 가다[갔다]

57 Track

What's your name?

~는 뭐야?

Say It! 무엇인지 물어볼 때
*What's는 What is을 줄인 말이에요.

Fill it! Listen to the track and fill in the blanks with the correct sentence number.

A.

B.

I.

H. April 28

What's ~?

C.

G.

F.

E. Mark

D.

501 What's your name?	**506** What's the date today?
502 What's your idea?	**507** What's the matter?
503 What's the answer?	**508** What's that noise?
504 What's the lunch menu?	**509** What's your favorite TV show?
505 What's the plan now?	

Study words & chunks!

⭐ Choose the correct words or chunks for each sentence and fill in the blanks. ▷

the matter

your idea

that noise

your name

your favorite TV show

the lunch menu

the plan

the answer

the date

501	What's _____ ?	(너의 이름)
502	What's _____ ?	(너의 생각)
503	What's _____ ?	(답)
504	What's _____ ?	(점심 메뉴)
505	What's _____ now?	(계획)
506	What's _____ today?	(날짜)
507	What's _____ ?	((걱정·고민 등의 원인이 되는) 문제)
508	What's _____ ?	(저 시끄러운 소리)
509	What's _____ ?	(네가 가장 좋아하는 TV 쇼)

Guess it!

⭐ In each picture, what would he or she most likely say?
Using '**What's ~?**' make a sentence with the words or chunks below.

the plan	your name	the answer
your favorite TV show	the matter	that noise
the lunch menu	your idea	the date

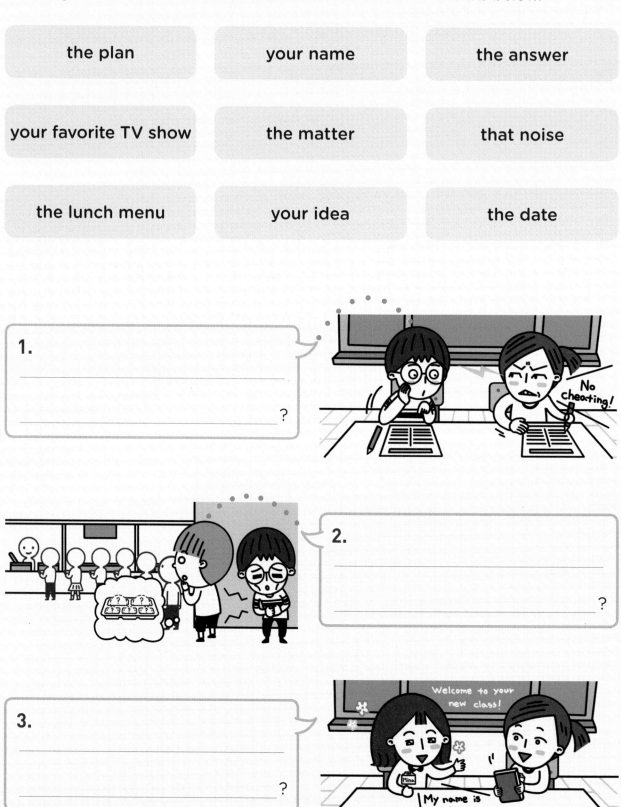

1.

_____

_____ ?

2.

_____

_____ ?

3.

_____

_____ ?

Speak Up!

⭐ Complete the dialogues with the best sentence from this track.

> **보기**
>
> **A:** I don't have enough money for her present.
>
> **B:** So, **what's the plan** now?
>
> **A:** Well, I think I can make something for her.

1

A: 🎤 _____ ▷ today?

B: It's July 13th.

A: Already? My mom's birthday is tomorrow!

Ⓡ

2

A: 🎤 _____ ▷ ?

B: It's coming from upstairs.

A: I can't hear the TV. It's so loud.

Ⓡ

3

A: Oh, no!

B: 🎤 _____ ▷ ?

A: I don't see my bike anywhere. I think somebody stole it!

Ⓡ

세이펜을 통해 각 상황에 맞는 말을 직접 녹음해보고 확실히 익혔는지 확인해보세요.

📖 **[보기]** something 무엇 **1.** July 7월 | 13th[thirteenth] (월의) 13일 **2.** upstairs 위층 | hear 듣다 | loud (소리가) 큰 **3.** bike 자전거 | anywhere 어디에서도 | somebody 누군가 | steal[stole] 훔치다[훔쳤다]

What do you need?

58
Track

너는 무엇을 ~하니(~해)?

Say It! 상대방의 상태나 행동에 대해 물어볼 때

Fill it! Listen to the track and fill in the blanks with the correct sentence number.

What do you ~?

I.   A.   B.   C.   H.   G.   F.   E.   D.

510 What do you need?	**515** What do you have in your hand?
511 What do you think?	**516** What do you hate the most?
512 What do you mean?	**517** What do you want to eat?
513 What do you do for fun?	**518** What do you feel like doing?
514 What do you like about her?	

Study words & chunks!

⭐ Choose the correct words or chunks for each sentence and fill in the blanks. ▶

think

feel like doing

do for fun

hate the most

mean

want to eat

need

like about her

have in your hand

510 What do you _____ ? (필요하다)

511 What do you _____ ? (생각하다)

512 What do you _____ ? (의미하다)

513 What do you _____ ? (재미를 위해 ~을 하다)

514 What do you _____ ? (그녀의 ~을 좋아하다)

515 What do you _____ ? (너의 손 안에 가지고 있다)

516 What do you _____ ? (가장 싫어하다)

517 What do you _____ ? (먹고 싶다)

518 What do you _____ ? (~을 하고 싶어 하다)

Guess it!

⭐ In each picture, what would he or she most likely say?
Using '**What do you ~?**' make a sentence with the words or chunks below.

mean	think	like about her
feel like doing	want to eat	hate the most
need	have in your hand	do for fun

1.
_____
_____?

2.
_____
_____?

3.
_____
_____?

Speak Up!

⭐ Complete the dialogues with the best sentence from this track.

> **보기**
>
> **A:** You look very different today.
>
> **B: What do you mean?**
>
> **A:** You don't usually wear a cap, but it looks good on you! I like it!

1

A: 🎤 _____ ▷?

B: I will get a cheeseburger. What about you?

A: I will have one, too.

Ⓡ

2

A: 🎤 _____ ▷?

B: I really don't like spiders. What about you?

A: I can't stand spiders either.

Ⓡ

3

A: 🎤 _____ ▷?

B: I love drawing pictures.

A: Really? Can I see your drawings?

Ⓡ

> 세이펜을 통해 각 상황에 맞는 말을 직접 녹음해
> 보고 확실히 익혔는지 확인해보세요.

📖 **[보기]** look ~해 보이다 ｜ usually 보통 ｜ look good on ~에게 잘 어울리다 **1.** cheeseburger 치즈버거 ｜ What about ~? ~은 어때? **2.** really 정말로 ｜ spider 거미 ｜ can't stand ~을 참을 수 없다 ｜ either ~도 역시 **3.** draw 그리다 ｜ drawing 그림

59 Track

What are you doing?

너는 무엇을 ～하고 있어?

Say It! 상대방에게 지금 뭘 하고 있는지 물어볼 때

Fill it! Listen to the track and fill in the blanks with the correct sentence number.

What are you -ing?

I.

A.

B.

C.

D.

E.

F.

G.

H.

519 What are you doing?	**524** What are you thinking about?
520 What are you eating?	**525** What are you waiting for?
521 What are you reading?	**526** What are you laughing at?
522 What are you looking at?	**527** What are you planning to do tomorrow?
523 What are you talking about?	

Study words & chunks!

⭐ Choose the correct words or chunks for each sentence and fill in the blanks. ▷

planning to do

doing

reading

looking at

thinking about

laughing at

eating

waiting for

talking about

519 What are you _____ ? (~을 하고 있는)

520 What are you _____ ? (~을 먹고 있는)

521 What are you _____ ? (~을 읽고 있는)

522 What are you _____ ? (~을 보고 있는)

523 What are you _____ ? (~에 대해 말하고 있는)

524 What are you _____ ? (~에 대해 생각하고 있는)

525 What are you _____ ? (~을 기다리고 있는)

526 What are you _____ ? (~에 대해 웃고 있는)

527 What are you _____ tomorrow? (~할 계획을 하고 있는)

Guess it!

⭐ In each picture, what would he or she most likely say?
Using '**What are you –ing?**' make a sentence with the words or chunks below.

planning to do	thinking about	reading
waiting for	eating	talking about
looking at	laughing at	doing

1.
_____
_____ ?

2.
_____
_____ ?

3.
_____
_____ ?

Speak Up!

⭐ Complete the dialogues with the best sentence from this track.

보기

> **A:** Our homework was easy, wasn't it?
>
> **B:** Homework? **What are you talking about**? Did we have homework?
>
> **A:** Yes, we did! Did you forget?

1

A: You look busy. 🎤 _____ ▷ ?

B: I'm making something for the next class.

A: You should put it away now. The class will start soon.

Ⓡ

2

A: 🎤 _____ ▷ ?

B: There is a little puppy over there. Do you see it?

A: Yes, it's so cute.

Ⓡ

3

A: Yay! Tomorrow is a holiday! 　　　　　　　*Yay! 야호!

B: 🎤 _____ ▷ tomorrow?

A: I'm going to eat out with my family.

Ⓡ

> 세이펜을 통해 각 상황에 맞는 말을 직접 녹음해
> 보고 확실히 익혔는지 확인해보세요.

📖 **[보기] 1.** something 무엇 | put away 치우다 | soon 곧　**2.** there is 〜이 있다 | over there 저쪽에
　3. am[are, is] going to 〜할 것이다 | eat out 외식하다

60 Track

Who is your best friend?

~은 누구야?

Say It! 어떤 사람이 누군지 물어볼 때

Fill it! Listen to the track and fill in the blanks with the correct sentence number.

H.

A.

B.

C.

Who is ~?

G.

F.

E.

D.

528 Who is your best friend?

529 Who is your class president?

530 Who is your homeroom teacher?

531 Who is the boy next to you?

532 Who is that boy over there?

533 Who is that girl with long hair?

534 Who is this girl in the picture?

535 Who is the boy in the red T-shirt?

Study words & chunks!

⭐ Choose the correct words or chunks for each sentence and fill in the blanks. ▷

this girl in the picture

your class president

the boy next to you

your best friend

that girl with long hair

your homeroom teacher

that boy over there

the boy in the red T-shirt

528 Who is _____ ? (너의 가장 친한 친구)

529 Who is _____ ? (너희 반장)

530 Who is _____ ? (너희 담임 선생님)

531 Who is _____ ? (네 옆에 있는 남자아이)

532 Who is _____ ? (저쪽에 있는 저 남자아이)

533 Who is _____ ? (긴 머리를 가진 저 여자아이)

534 Who is _____ ? (사진 속의 이 여자아이)

535 Who is _____ ? (빨간 티셔츠를 입은 남자아이)

Guess it!

⭐ In each picture, what would he or she most likely say?
Using '**Who is ~?**' make a sentence with the words or chunks below.

your class president	the boy in the red T-shirt	the boy next to you
this girl in the picture	your best friend	that girl with long hair
	that boy over there	your homeroom teacher

1.

_____

_____ **?**

2.

_____

_____ **?**

3.

_____

_____ **?**

Speak Up!

⭐ Complete the dialogues with the best sentence from this track.

보기

A: I took a picture in the amusement park!

B: Let me see. **Who is this girl in the picture**?

A: Oh, she is my sister.

1

A: 🎤 _____ ▷ ?

B: He is my brother. That color is his favorite.

A: I guess so. He's wearing red shoes too!   *I guess so. 그런 것 같아.   Ⓡ

2

A: 🎤 _____ ▷ ?

B: That boy by the door. He got the most votes.   Ⓡ

3

A: I'm writing a letter to my best friend.

B: 🎤 _____ ▷ ?

A: Her name is Lucy. She is in class 5.   Ⓡ

세이펜을 통해 각 상황에 맞는 말을 직접 녹음해 보고 확실히 익혔는지 확인해보세요.

📖 **[보기]** take[took] a picture 사진을 찍다[찍었다] | amusement park 놀이공원 | let me 내가 ~할게 **1.** so 그렇게 **2.** get[got] 얻다[얻었다] | most 가장 많은 | vote 표, 투표 **3.** Lucy 루시(여자 이름)

Why do you say that?

너는 왜 ~해?

Say It! 상대방에게 어떤 행동을 왜 하는지 물어볼 때

Fill it! Listen to the track and fill in the blanks with the correct sentence number.

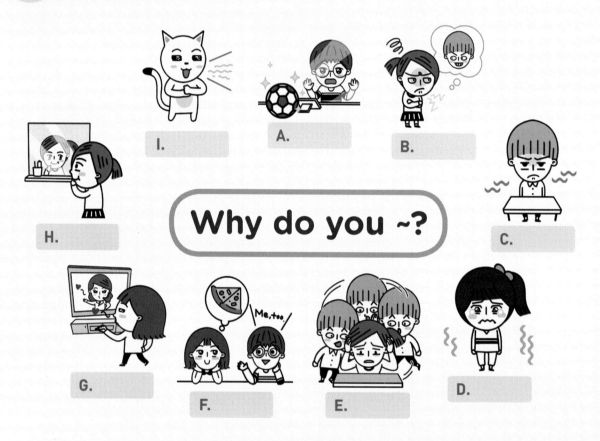

Why do you ~?

536 Why do you say that?	**541** Why do you get upset?
537 Why do you like the singer?	**542** Why do you want to have it?
538 Why do you hate him?	**543** Why do you keep looking in the mirror?
539 Why do you think so?	
540 Why do you look so sad?	**544** Why do you keep bothering me?

Study words & chunks!

⭐ Choose the correct words or chunks for each sentence and fill in the blanks. ▷

hate him

like the singer

want to have it

get upset

say that

think so

look so sad

keep bothering me

keep looking
in the mirror

536	Why do you _____ ?	(그것을 말하다)
537	Why do you _____ ?	(그 가수를 좋아하다)
538	Why do you _____ ?	(그를 싫어하다)
539	Why do you _____ ?	(그렇게 생각하다)
540	Why do you _____ ?	(매우 슬퍼 보이다)
541	Why do you _____ ?	(속이 상하다)
542	Why do you _____ ?	(그것을 가지고 싶어 하다)
543	Why do you _____ ?	(거울을 계속 들여다보다)
544	Why do you _____ ?	(나를 계속 귀찮게 하다)

Guess it!

⭐ In each picture, what would he or she most likely say?
Using '**Why do you ~?**' make a sentence with the words or chunks below.

keep bothering me	look so sad	like the singer
think so	keep looking in the mirror	say that
get upset	want to have it	hate him

1.

_____

_____ ?

2.

_____

_____ ?

3.

_____

_____ ?

Speak Up!

⭐ Complete the dialogues with the best sentence from this track.

> **보기**
>
> **A:** I think it will rain soon.
>
> **B:** <u>Why do you think so</u>?
>
> **A:** It's starting to get dark. It's very cloudy too.

1

A: 🎤 _____ ▷ ?

B: I'm checking my bangs. I think they are too short.

A: Don't worry about it. Your bangs are just fine.   Ⓡ

2

A: 🎤 _____ ▷ ?

B: My dog is really sick, so she's in the hospital now.

A: That's too bad.   *That's too bad. 그것 참 안됐다.   Ⓡ

3

A: I want this comic book for my birthday.

B: 🎤 _____ ▷ ?

A: It's the final one of my favorite comic book series.   Ⓡ

세이펜을 통해 각 상황에 맞는 말을 직접 녹음해
보고 확실히 익혔는지 확인해보세요.

📖 **[보기]** soon 곧 | start to ~하기 시작하다 | get dark 어두워지다 | cloudy 흐린, 구름이 많은 **1.** bangs 앞머리
3. comic book 만화책 | final 마지막의 | series 시리즈

62 Track

Why don't we go outside?

우리 ~하는 게 어때(~하지 않을래)?

Say It! 상대방에게 어떤 행동을 같이 하자고 제안할 때

Fill it! Listen to the track and fill in the blanks with the correct sentence number.

Why don't we ~?

545 Why don't we go outside?

546 Why don't we go together?

547 Why don't we share?

548 Why don't we ride bikes?

549 Why don't we watch a movie?

550 Why don't we ask our teacher?

551 Why don't we have some ice cream?

552 Why don't we switch seats?

553 Why don't we meet on Thursday?

Study words & chunks!

⭐ Choose the correct words or chunks for each sentence and fill in the blanks. ▷

meet

have some ice cream

go together

ride bikes

switch seats

ask our teacher

go outside

watch a movie

share

545 Why don't we _____ ? (밖으로 나가다)

546 Why don't we _____ ? (같이 가다)

547 Why don't we _____ ? (같이 쓰다)

548 Why don't we _____ ? (자전거를 타다)

549 Why don't we _____ ? (영화를 보다)

550 Why don't we _____ ? (선생님께 여쭤보다)

551 Why don't we _____ ? (아이스크림을 먹다)

552 Why don't we _____ ? (자리를 바꾸다)

553 Why don't we _____ on Thursday? (만나다)

Guess it!

⭐ In each picture, what would he or she most likely say?
Using '**Why don't we ~?**' make a sentence with the words or chunks below.

go outside	switch seats	share
ask our teacher	go together	have some ice cream
ride bikes	meet	watch a movie

1.
_____
_____ ?

2.
_____
_____ ?

3.
_____
_____ ?

Speak Up!

⭐ Complete the dialogues with the best sentence from this track.

> **A:** <u>**Why don't we meet**</u> on Thursday?
>
> **B:** I have another plan that day. How about Friday?
>
> **A:** Okay.

1

A: You don't look good. What's wrong?

B: I feel sick. I always get sick on the bus.

A: 🎤 _____ ▷ ? It could help.

Ⓡ

2

A: 🎤 _____ ▷ ?

B: I'd like to, but I can't. I don't have a bike.

A: I have two. You can ride one of mine.

Ⓡ

3

A: She is absent today. What happened to her?

B: I don't know. 🎤 _____ ▷ ?

A: Okay.

Ⓡ

> 세이펜을 통해 각 상황에 맞는 말을 직접 녹음해
> 보고 확실히 익혔는지 확인해보세요.

📖 **[보기]** How about ~? ~은 어때? | Friday 금요일 **1.** look ~해 보이다 | feel sick 속이 안 좋다 **2.** would['d] like to ~하고 싶다 | mine 내 것 **3.** absent 결석한 | happen[happened] (일이) 일어나다[일어났다]

Where is my umbrella?

63
Track

~는 어디에 있어?

Say It! 어떤 사람이나 무언가가 어디에 있는지 물어볼 때

Fill it! Listen to the track and fill in the blanks with the correct sentence number.

I.

A.

B.

H.

Where is ~?

C.

G.

F.

E.

D.

554 Where is Mom?

559 Where is my green T-shirt?

555 Where is your school?

560 Where is that grape juice?

556 Where is your house?

561 Where is the bathroom?

557 Where is my umbrella?

562 Where is the bus stop?

558 Where is my backpack?

Study words & chunks!

⭐ Choose the correct words or chunks for each sentence and fill in the blanks. ▷

your house

my green T-shirt

that grape juice

the bathroom

the bus stop

my backpack

my umbrella

Mom

your school

554 Where is _____? (엄마)

555 Where is _____? (너의 학교)

556 Where is _____? (너의 집)

557 Where is _____? (내 우산)

558 Where is _____? (내 책가방)

559 Where is _____? (내 초록색 티셔츠)

560 Where is _____? (그 포도 주스)

561 Where is _____? (화장실)

562 Where is _____? (버스 정류장)

Guess it!

⭐ In each picture, what would he or she most likely say?
Using '**Where is ~?**' make a sentence with the words or chunks below.

the bathroom	my green T-shirt	your house
my umbrella	the bus stop	that grape juice
your school	Mom	my backpack

1.
_____
_____ ?

2.
_____
_____ ?

3.
_____
_____ ?

Speak Up!

⭐ Complete the dialogues with the best sentence from this track.

> **A: Where is my umbrella**?
>
> **B:** Did you check the basket by the door?
>
> **A:** I did, but it's not there. I'm going to get wet!

1

A: 🎤 _____ ▷ ?

B: She went to the market. She will be back soon.

Ⓡ

2

A: 🎤 _____ ▷ ?

B: Sorry, but I drank it all.

A: Oh, then I will just drink some water instead.

Ⓡ

3

A: I bought a new game. Do you want to come over and play?

B: Sure. 🎤 _____ ▷ ?   *Sure. 물론이지.

A: It's really close to our school.

Ⓡ

> 세이펜을 통해 각 상황에 맞는 말을 직접 녹음해 보고 확실히 익혔는지 확인해보세요.

📖 **[보기]** am[are, is] going to ~할 것이다 | get wet 물에 젖다 **1.** go[went] 가다[갔다] | soon 곧 **2.** drink [drank] 마시다[마셨다] | then 그러면 | instead 대신에 **3.** buy[bought] 사다[샀다] | want to ~하고 싶다 | close to ~에 가까운

64
Track

Where did you buy it?

너는 어디에서 ~했어?

Say It! 상대방이 예전에 무엇을 어디에서 했는지 물어볼 때

Fill it! Listen to the track and fill in the blanks with the correct sentence number.

I.

A.

B.

H.

Where did you ~?

C.

G.

F.

E.

D.

563 Where did you see me?

564 Where did you buy it?

565 Where did you find it?

566 Where did you put the ball?

567 Where did you learn Taekwondo?

568 Where did you hear that?

569 Where did you go for vacation?

570 Where did you take this picture?

571 Where did you lose your umbrella?

⭐ Choose the correct words or chunks for each sentence and fill in the blanks. ▷

see me

put the ball

buy it

hear that

lose your umbrella

learn Taekwondo

go for vacation

find it

take this picture

563 Where did you _____ ? (나를 보다)

564 Where did you _____ ? (그것을 사다)

565 Where did you _____ ? (그것을 찾다)

566 Where did you _____ ? (공을 놓다)

567 Where did you _____ ? (태권도를 배우다)

568 Where did you _____ ? (그것을 듣다)

569 Where did you _____ ? (휴가를 가다)

570 Where did you _____ ? (이 사진을 찍다)

571 Where did you _____ ? (너의 우산을 잃어버리다)

Guess it!

⭐ In each picture, what would he or she most likely say?
Using '**Where did you ~?**' make a sentence with the words or chunks below.

learn Taekwondo	hear that	lose your umbrella
put the ball	buy it	find it
go for vacation	take this picture	see me

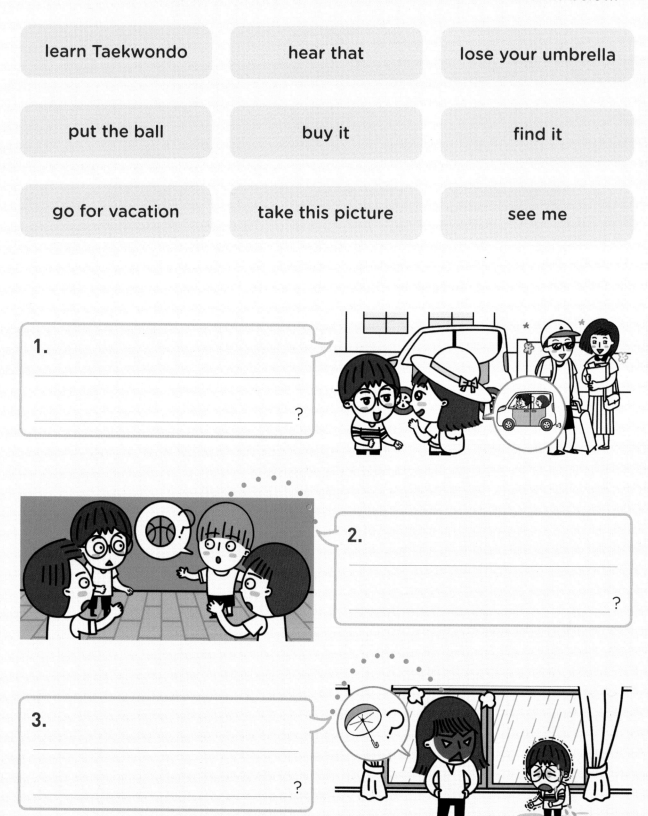

1. _____ ?

2. _____ ?

3. _____ ?

Speak Up!

⭐ Complete the dialogues with the best sentence from this track.

보기

> **A:** I like your new pencil case. **Where did you buy it**?
>
> **B:** My aunt bought it for me. It was a gift.

1

A: We can leave early today!

B: Are you sure? 🎤 _____ ▷ ?

A: My teacher told me in the morning.

Ⓡ

2

A: 🎤 _____ ▷ ? The color of

the sea is awesome!

B: In Jeju Island. I went there with my family.

Ⓡ

3

A: 🎤 _____ ▷ ?

B: I took an after-school class. It was a lot of fun!

Ⓡ

세이펜을 통해 각 상황에 맞는 말을 직접 녹음해
보고 확실히 익혔는지 확인해보세요.

📖 **[보기]** pencil case 필통 | buy[bought] 사 주다[사 주었다] **1.** leave 떠나다 | sure 확실한 | tell[told] 말하다[말했다] **2.** awesome 굉장한, 아주 멋진 | Jeju Island 제주도 | go[went] 가다[갔다] **3.** take[took] (수업을) 받다[받았다] | after-school class 방과 후 수업 | a lot of 많이, 많은

How do you do that?

너는 어떻게 ~해?

Say It! 상대방이 무엇을 어떻게 하는지 물어볼 때

Fill It! Listen to the track and fill in the blanks with the correct sentence number.

I.

A.

B.

How do you ~?

C.

H.

G.

F.

E.

D.

572 How do you feel?

573 How do you do that?

574 How do you get there?

575 How do you play this game?

576 How do you make new friends?

577 How do you turn this on?

578 How do you get such good grades?

579 How do you spend your free time?

580 How do you spend your allowance?

Study words & chunks!

⭐ Choose the correct words or chunks for each sentence and fill in the blanks. ▷

turn this on

feel

get there

do that

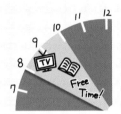

spend your free time

get such good grades

spend your allowance

play this game

make new friends

572	How do you _____ ?	(느끼다)
573	How do you _____ ?	(그것을 하다)
574	How do you _____ ?	(그곳에 가다, 그곳에 도착하다)
575	How do you _____ ?	(이 게임을 하다)
576	How do you _____ ?	(새로운 친구들을 사귀다)
577	How do you _____ ?	(이것을 켜다)
578	How do you _____ ?	(그렇게 좋은 성적을 받다)
579	How do you _____ ?	(너의 자유 시간을 보내다)
580	How do you _____ ?	(너의 용돈을 쓰다)

Guess it!

⭐ In each picture, what would he or she most likely say?
Using '**How do you ~?**' make a sentence with the words or chunks below.

feel	spend your free time	get there
play this game	make new friends	turn this on
get such good grades	do that	spend your allowance

1.
_____
_____ ?

2.
_____
_____ ?

3.
_____
_____ ?

Speak Up!

⭐ Complete the dialogues with the best sentence from this track.

> **A:** Is it a new game?
>
> **B:** Yes. It's easy and fun. Here, you can try it.
>
> **A:** **How do you play this game**?

1

A: 🎤 _____ ▷ ?

B: I feel better now. I went to the doctor yesterday.

A: I'm glad to hear that.

Ⓡ

2

A: 🎤 _____ ▷ ?

B: I usually play games. How about you?

A: I enjoy watching TV with my family.

Ⓡ

3

A: 🎤 _____ ▷ ?

B: I always say hi first. And I show my interest in their favorite things.

A: Oh, that's good. I'll try that.

Ⓡ

세이펜을 통해 각 상황에 맞는 말을 직접 녹음해 보고 확실히 익혔는지 확인해보세요.

📖 **[보기]** try 해 보다 **1.** feel better 몸[기분]이 나아지다 | hear 듣다 | go[went] to the doctor 병원에 가다[갔다] **2.** usually 보통 | How about ~? ~은 어때? **3.** say hi 인사하다 | first 먼저 | show interest in ~에 관심을 보이다

정답과 해설 p.14

When are you going to come?

너는 언제 ~할 거야?

Say It! 상대방에게 무엇을 언제 할 건지 물어볼 때

 Fill it! Listen to the track and fill in the blanks with the correct sentence number.

I.

A.

B.

H.

When are you going to ~?

C.

G.

F.

E.

D.

581 When are you going to come?

582 When are you going to start?

583 When are you going to be ready?

584 When are you going to see her?

585 When are you going to tell her?

586 When are you going to be free?

587 When are you going to take a break?

588 When are you going to leave?

589 When are you going to bring it back?

Study words & chunks!

⭐ Choose the correct words or chunks for each sentence and fill in the blanks. ▷

be ready

see her

leave

take a break

tell her

come

start

bring it back

be free

581 When are you going to _____	?	(오다)
582 When are you going to _____	?	(시작하다)
583 When are you going to _____	?	(준비되다)
584 When are you going to _____	?	(그녀를 만나다)
585 When are you going to _____	?	(그녀에게 말하다)
586 When are you going to _____	?	(시간이 나다)
587 When are you going to _____	?	(잠시 쉬다)
588 When are you going to _____	?	(떠나다, 출발하다)
589 When are you going to _____	?	(그것을 돌려주다)

Guess it!

⭐ In each picture, what would he or she most likely say?
　　Using '**When are you going to ~?**' make a sentence with the words or chunks below.

tell her	leave	come
be ready	bring it back	start
be free	take a break	see her

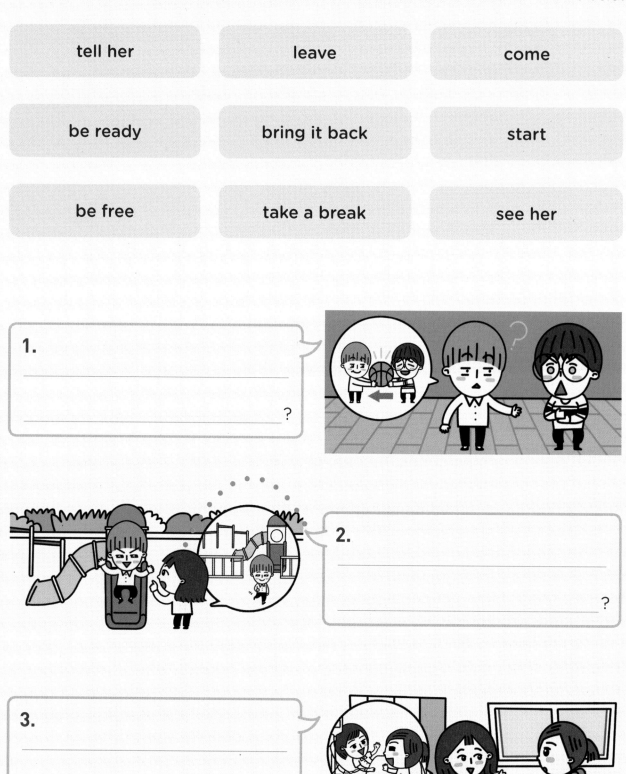

1.

_____

_____ ?

2.

_____

_____ ?

3.

_____

_____ ?

Speak Up!

⭐ Complete the dialogues with the best sentence from this track.

> **보기**
>
> **A:** Can we talk about it now?
>
> **B:** I'm sorry, but I have to finish this first.
>
> **A:** **When are you going to be free**? I will call you then.

1

A: Did you tell your mom about the broken window?

B: Not yet. I'm afraid.

A: 🎤 _____ ▷ ?

You should do it soon.

Ⓡ

2

A: 🎤 _____ ▷ ?

We should hurry.

B: I'm almost ready. Give me a second.   *Give me a second. 잠깐만 시간을 줘.

Ⓡ

3

A: I'm going to take guitar lessons.

B: That's cool. 🎤 _____ ▷ ?

A: Next month. I'm really excited.

Ⓡ

세이펜을 통해 각 상황에 맞는 말을 직접 녹음해
보고 확실히 익혔는지 확인해보세요.

📖 **[보기]** have to ～해야 한다 | first 먼저 | then 그때 **1.** broken 깨진 | soon 빨리 **2.** second (아주) 잠깐 **3.** am[are, is] going to ～할 것이다 | take lessons 수업을 받다 | guitar 기타 | cool 멋진 | really 정말로 | excited 신이 난

67

Track

What a cool gift!

정말 ~이다(하다)!

Say it! 감탄을 표현할 때

Fill it! Listen to the track and fill in the blanks with the correct sentence number.

A.

B.

H.

What ~!

C.

G.

F.

E.

D.

590 What a great idea!

591 What a poor cat!

592 What a cool gift!

593 What a surprise!

594 What a mess!

595 What an amazing story!

596 What a disappointment!

597 What a silly thing to say!

Study words & chunks!

⭐ Choose the correct words or chunks for each sentence and fill in the blanks. ▷

a poor cat

a mess

an amazing story

a silly thing to say

a surprise

a great idea

a cool gift

a disappointment

590	What	!	(훌륭한 생각)
591	What	!	(불쌍한 고양이)
592	What	!	(멋진 선물)
593	What	!	(놀라운 일)
594	What	!	(엉망진창)
595	What	!	(굉장한 이야기)
596	What	!	(실망스러운 것[사람])
597	What	!	(어리석은 말)

Guess it!

⭐ In each picture, what would he or she most likely say?
Using '**What ~!**' make a sentence with the words or chunks below.

> a cool gift   an amazing story   a great idea
>
> a mess   a disappointment   a surprise
>
> a poor cat   a silly thing to say

1.

_____

_____ !

2.

_____

_____ !

3.

_____

_____ !

Speak Up!

⭐ Complete the dialogues with the best sentence from this track.

> **보기**
>
> **A:** We have so much homework during the vacation.
>
> **B: What a disappointment**! Can you do all of it?
>
> **A:** I'm not sure. But I'll try.

1

A: 🎤 _____ ▷! There are things everywhere!

B: I know. I'll clean up soon.   *I know. 맞아.

A: Mom will be home soon. You should do it now.   Ⓡ

2

A: Her birthday is coming.

B: Yes, it is. Why don't we surprise her with a gift?

A: 🎤 _____ ▷! Let's make a plan.   Ⓡ

3

A: Did you finish reading that book?

B: Yes! 🎤 _____ ▷!

A: I know. I just couldn't wait to turn the page.   Ⓡ

> 세이펜을 통해 각 상황에 맞는 말을 직접 녹음해
> 보고 확실히 익혔는지 확인해보세요.

📖 **[보기]** vacation 방학 | sure 확실한 **1.** there are ~이 있다 | everywhere 모든 곳에 | clean up 치우다 | soon 곧 **2.** Why don't we ~? 우리 ~하는 게 어때? | surprise 놀라게 하다 | let's ~하자 | make a plan 계획을 세우다 **3.** can't[couldn't] wait to 빨리 ~하고 싶어 하다[싶어 했다] | turn (페이지를) 넘기다

68

Track

Be careful!

~해라(~해).

Say it! 상대방에게 뭔가를 하라고 지시하거나 명령할 때
*이때 문장은 Be careful!이나 Hurry up!처럼 바로 동사로 시작해요.

Fill it! Listen to the track and fill in the blanks with the correct sentence number.

H.

I.

A.

B.

C.

G.

F.

E.

D.

598 Hurry up!		**603** Come with me.
599 Be careful!		**604** Give it back to me.
600 Look at this!		**605** Leave me alone.
601 Wait a minute.		**606** Keep going.
602 Do it this way.		

Study words & chunks!

⭐ Choose the correct words or chunks for each sentence and fill in the blanks. ▷

wait a minute

hurry up

look at this

give it back to me

do it this way

leave me alone

be careful

keep going

come with me

598	_____ ! (서두르다)
599	_____ ! (조심하다)
600	_____ ! (이것을 보다)
601	_____ . (잠깐 기다리다)
602	_____ . (그것을 이렇게 하다)
603	_____ . (나와 함께 가다)
604	_____ . (나에게 그것을 돌려주다)
605	_____ . (나를 혼자 내버려 두다)
606	_____ . (계속하다, 계속 가다)

Guess it!

⭐ In each picture, what would he or she most likely say?

Give it back to me	Look at this	Wait a minute
Be careful	Leave me alone	Hurry up
Do it this way	Come with me	Keep going

1.
_____
_____ !

A movie?

Cinema

2.
_____
_____ .

3.
_____
_____ !

Speak Up!

⭐ Complete the dialogues with the best sentence from this track.

보기

A: Are you sure this is the right way? I'm confused.

B: Yes. **Keep going**. We are almost there.

1

A: Can I come over to your house?

B: Let me ask my mom first. 🎤 _____ ▷.

A: Okay.

Ⓡ

2

A: Are you ready to go out?

B: No. I have to change my clothes.

A: 🎤 _____ ▷! We don't have enough time.

Ⓡ

3

A: That is my diary! Why do you have it?

B: I just picked it up.

A: 🎤 _____ ▷. Did you read it?

Ⓡ

세이펜을 통해 각 상황에 맞는 말을 직접 녹음해 보고 확실히 익혔는지 확인해보세요.

📖 **[보기]** sure 확실한 | confused 헷갈리는 **1.** come over to (다른 사람의 집에) 가다 | let me 내가 ~하게 해줘 | first 먼저 **2.** ready to ~할 준비가 된 | have to ~해야 한다 | change (옷을) 갈아입다 **3.** pick[picked] up 줍다[주웠다]

69 Track

Don't worry.

～하지 마.

Say It! 뭔가를 하지 말라고 말할 때
*Don't는 Do not을 줄인 말이에요.

Fill it! Listen to the track and fill in the blanks with the correct sentence number.

Don't ~.

I.

A.

B.

C.

H.

G.

F.

E.

D.

607 Don't worry.

608 Don't tell anybody.

609 Don't call me that.

610 Don't bother me.

611 Don't be scared.

612 Don't cut in line.

613 Don't make me angry.

614 Don't make fun of me.

615 Don't forget to bring it back.

Study words & chunks!

⭐ Choose the correct words or chunks for each sentence and fill in the blanks. ▷

bother me

make fun of me

cut in line

be scared

make me angry

worry

forget to bring it back

tell anybody

call me that

607 Don't _____. (걱정하다)

608 Don't _____. (누군가에게 말하다)

609 Don't _____. (나를 그렇게 부르다)

610 Don't _____. (나를 귀찮게 하다)

611 Don't _____. (무서워하다)

612 Don't _____. (새치기하다)

613 Don't _____. (나를 화나게 하다)

614 Don't _____. (나를 놀리다)

615 Don't _____. (그것을 돌려주는 것을 잊어버리다)

Guess it!

⭐ In each picture, what would he or she most likely say?
Using '**Don't ~.**' make a sentence with the words or chunks below.

tell anybody	forget to bring it back	cut in line
worry	call me that	be scared
make fun of me	bother me	make me angry

1.
_____
_____.

2.
_____
_____.

It's a secret.

3.
_____
_____.

I'm busy.

Speak Up!

⭐ Complete the dialogues with the best sentence from this track.

> **보기**
>
> **A:** Your dog is very big.
>
> **B: Don't be scared.** He doesn't bite.
>
> **A:** I'm not scared. I'm just a little surprised.

1

A: There are so many people in line.

B: Oh, I see my friend at the front. Maybe we can stand behind him.

A: 🎤 _____ ▷. That's not fair. Ⓡ

2

A: Can I borrow your art textbook?

B: Sure, but 🎤 _____ ▷. *Sure. 물론이지.

I need it tomorrow. Ⓡ

3

A: I saw when you slipped on the ice. It was funny.

B: 🎤 _____ ▷. It really hurt! Ⓡ

> 세이펜을 통해 각 상황에 맞는 말을 직접 녹음해
> 보고 확실히 익혔는지 확인해보세요.

📖 **[보기]** a little 조금, 약간 | surprised 놀란 **1.** there are ~이 있다 | fair 공평한, 공정한 **3.** see[saw] 보다[보았다] | slip[slipped] 미끄러지다[미끄러졌다] | funny 웃기는 | really 정말로 | hurt[hurt] 아프다[아팠다]

70 Track

Let's meet at five.

～하자.

Say It! 다른 사람에게 함께 무엇을 하자고 말할 때

Fill it! Listen to the track and fill in the blanks with the correct sentence number.

Let's ~.

I.

A.

B.

H.

C.

G.

F.

E.

D.

616 Let's go outside.

617 Let's play a game.

618 Let's meet at five.

619 Let's take a break.

620 Let's do it quickly.

621 Let's have lunch together.

622 Let's get started.

623 Let's get together tomorrow.

624 Let's go back to the classroom.

Study words & chunks!

⭐ Choose the correct words or chunks for each sentence and fill in the blanks. ▷

meet at five

get started

do it quickly

go back to the classroom

get together

take a break

play a game

have lunch together

go outside

616 Let's _____. (밖으로 나가다)

617 Let's _____. (게임하다)

618 Let's _____. (다섯 시에 만나다)

619 Let's _____. (잠시 쉬다)

620 Let's _____. (그것을 빨리하다)

621 Let's _____. (점심을 함께 먹다)

622 Let's _____. (시작하다)

623 Let's _____ tomorrow. (만나다, 모이다)

624 Let's _____. (교실로 돌아가다)

Guess it!

⭐ In each picture, what would he or she most likely say?
Using '**Let's ~.**' make a sentence with the words or chunks below.

play a game	take a break	go back to the classroom
have lunch together	get together	go outside
get started	meet at five	do it quickly

1.
_____
_____ .

2.
_____
_____ .

3.
_____
_____ .

Speak Up!

⭐ Complete the dialogues with the best sentence from this track.

보기

> A: We have to start our group homework.
>
> B: Can we do it later? I don't want to do it now.
>
> A: Come on! **Let's do it quickly**. We can play after that.

1

A: I'm so bored. Do you have anything fun to do?

B: 🎤 _____ ▷.

A: Great! What kind of game is it?

Ⓡ

2

A: Did she invite you to her birthday party?

B: Yes. But I don't know how to get there.

A: We can go together. 🎤 _____ ▷.

Ⓡ

3

A: Come on. The class is about to start.

B: But I want to go to the bathroom.

A: We don't have enough time.

🎤 _____ ▷.

Ⓡ

세이펜을 통해 각 상황에 맞는 말을 직접 녹음해
보고 확실히 익혔는지 확인해보세요.

📖 **[보기]** have to ~해야 한다 | later 나중에 | want to ~하고 싶다 **1.** bored 지루한 | anything 무엇인가
2. invite A to B A를 B에 초대하다 | how to ~하는 방법 **3.** is[am, are] about to 막 ~하려는 참이다

memo ✎

memo ✍

memo ✑

EGU

THE EASIEST GRAMMAR & USAGE

EGU 시리즈 소개

EGU
서술형 기초 세우기

영단어&품사
서술형·문법의 기초가 되는
영단어와 품사 결합 학습

문장 형식
기본 동사 32개를 활용한
문장 형식별 학습

동사 써먹기
기본 동사 24개를 활용한
확장식 문장 쓰기 연습

EGU
서술형·문법 다지기

문법 써먹기
개정 교육 과정
중1 서술형·문법 완성

구문 써먹기
개정 교육 과정
중2, 중3 서술형·문법 완성

쎄듀

완벽한 영어 수업을 위한 **AI 파트너!**

쎄듀런 OPEN

저작권 걱정 없는
쎄듀 오리지널 콘텐츠 여기 다 있다!

8만
문법·서술형
문항

2만
구문 문장

2만
어휘

총 120,000 DB를
쎄듀런에서!

www.cedulearn.com

1 구문
판매 1위 '천일문' 콘텐츠를 활용하여 정확하고 다양한 구문 학습

(끊어읽기) (해석하기) (문장 구조 분석) (해설·해석 제공) (단어 스크램블링) (영작하기)

2 문법·서술형
쎄듀의 모든 문법 문항을 활용하여 내신까지 해결하는 정교한 문법 유형 제공

(객관식과 주관식의 결합) (문법 포인트별 학습) (보기를 활용한 집합 문항) (내신대비 서술형) (어법+서술형 문제)

3 어휘
초·중·고·공무원까지 방대한 어휘량을 제공하며 오프라인 TEST 인쇄도 가능

(영단어 카드 학습) (단어 ↔ 뜻 유형) (예문 활용 유형) (단어 매칭 게임)

4 선생님 보유 문항 이용

(Online Test) (OMR Test)

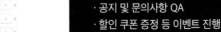
🍵 cafe.naver.com/cedulearnteacher

쎄듀런 학습 정보가 궁금하다면?
쎄듀런 Cafe

· 쎄듀런 사용법 안내 & 학습법 공유
· 공지 및 문의사항 QA
· 할인 쿠폰 증정 등 이벤트 진행

초 등 코 치

천일문

sentence

• • •

WORKBOOK

with 세이펜

3

천일문
sentence

◆ ◆ ◆

WORKBOOK

3

49
Track

I'm going to play outside.

나는 ~할 거야.

Master words & chunks!

Ⓐ 상자 안에 있는 단어 조각들을 화살표로 연결하여 이번 트랙에서 배운 표현을 만들어 보세요.

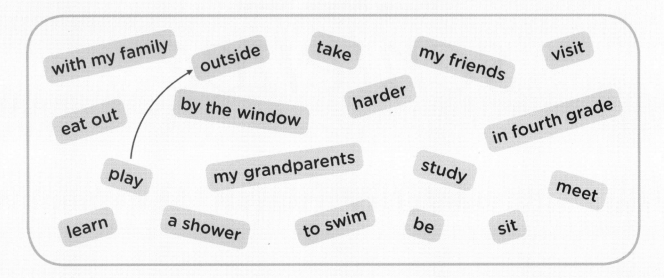

Ⓑ 상자에서 연결한 표현을 다시 한 번 써보고 뜻을 적어보세요.

Words & Chunks	뜻

Master sentences!

⭐ 앞에서 복습한 표현을 사용하여 이번 트랙에서 배운 문장을 각 그림에 맞게 완성해보세요.

나는 ~할 거야.

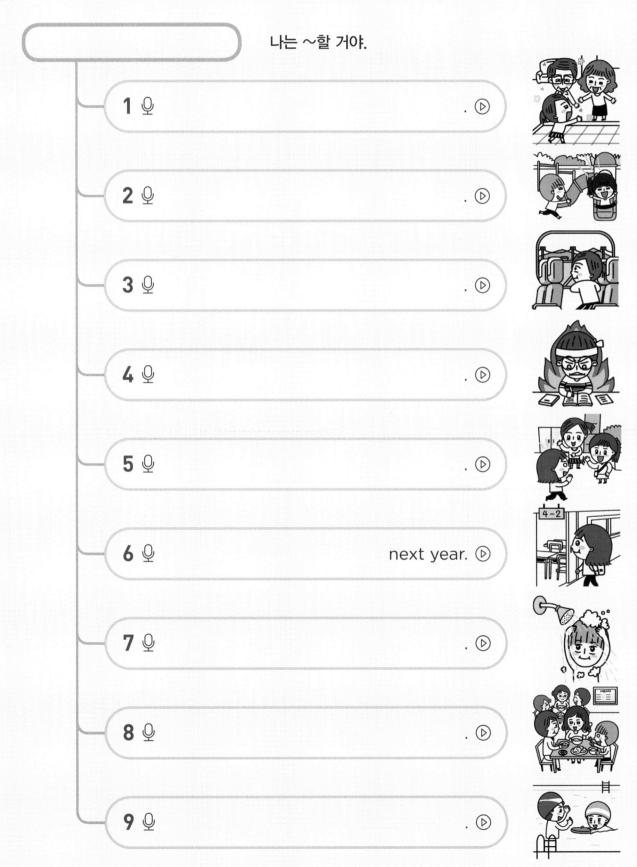

1 🎤 . ▷

2 🎤 . ▷

3 🎤 . ▷

4 🎤 . ▷

5 🎤 . ▷

6 🎤 next year. ▷

7 🎤 . ▷

8 🎤 . ▷

9 🎤 . ▷

50
Track

He's going to be fine.

그[그녀]는 ~할 거야.

Master words & chunks!

Ⓐ 상자 안에 있는 단어 조각들을 화살표로 연결하여 이번 트랙에서 배운 표현을 만들어 보세요.

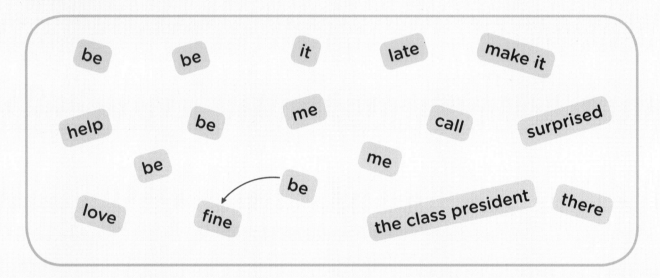

Ⓑ 상자에서 연결한 표현과 남는 단어 조각을 다시 한 번 써보고 뜻을 적어보세요.

Words & Chunks	뜻

Master sentences!

⭐ 앞에서 복습한 표현을 사용하여 이번 트랙에서 배운 문장을 각 그림에 맞게 완성해보세요.

그는 ～할 거야.

1 🎤　　　　　　　　　　　　　　　．▷

2 🎤　　　　　　　　　　　　　　　．▷

3 🎤　　　　　　　　　　　　　　　．▷

4 🎤　　　　　　　　　　　　　　　．▷

그녀는 ～할 거야.

5 🎤　　　　　　　　　　　　　　　．▷

6 🎤　　　　　　　　　　　　　　　．▷

7 🎤　　　　　　　　　　　　　　　．▷

8 🎤　　　　　　　　　　　　　　　．▷

9 🎤　　　　　　　　　　　　　　　．▷

51 Track

Are you going to say yes?

너는 ~할 거야?

Master words & chunks!

ⓐ 상자 안에 있는 단어 조각들을 화살표로 연결하여 이번 트랙에서 배운 표현을 만들어 보세요.

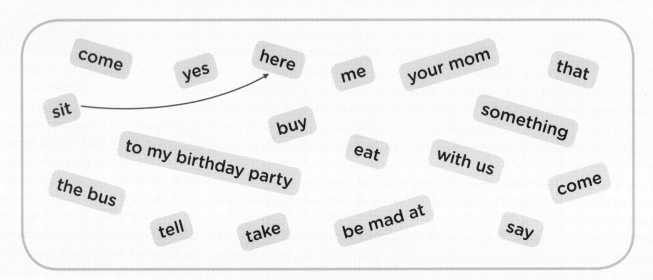

ⓑ 상자에서 연결한 표현을 다시 한 번 써보고 뜻을 적어보세요.

Words & Chunks	뜻

Master sentences!

⭐ 앞에서 복습한 표현을 사용하여 이번 트랙에서 배운 문장을 각 그림에 맞게 완성해보세요.

너는 ~할 거야?

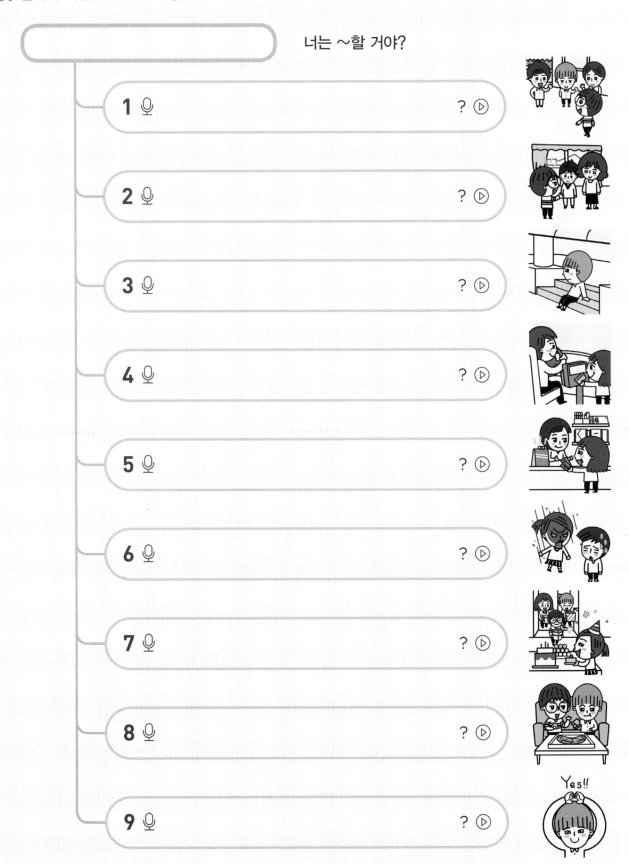

1 🎤 ? ▷

2 🎤 ? ▷

3 🎤 ? ▷

4 🎤 ? ▷

5 🎤 ? ▷

6 🎤 ? ▷

7 🎤 ? ▷

8 🎤 ? ▷

9 🎤 ? ▷

52
Track

I was about to tell you.

나는 막 ~하려던 참이었어.

Master words & chunks!

Ⓐ 상자 안에 있는 단어 조각들을 화살표로 연결하여 이번 트랙에서 배운 표현을 만들어 보세요.

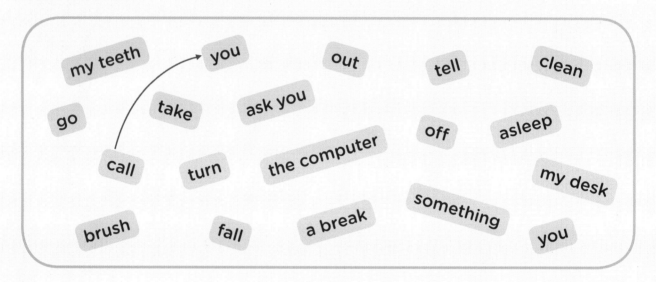

Ⓑ 상자에서 연결한 표현을 다시 한 번 써보고 뜻을 적어보세요.

Words & Chunks	뜻

Master sentences!

★ 앞에서 복습한 표현을 사용하여 이번 트랙에서 배운 문장을 각 그림에 맞게 완성해보세요.

나는 막 ~하려던 참이었어.

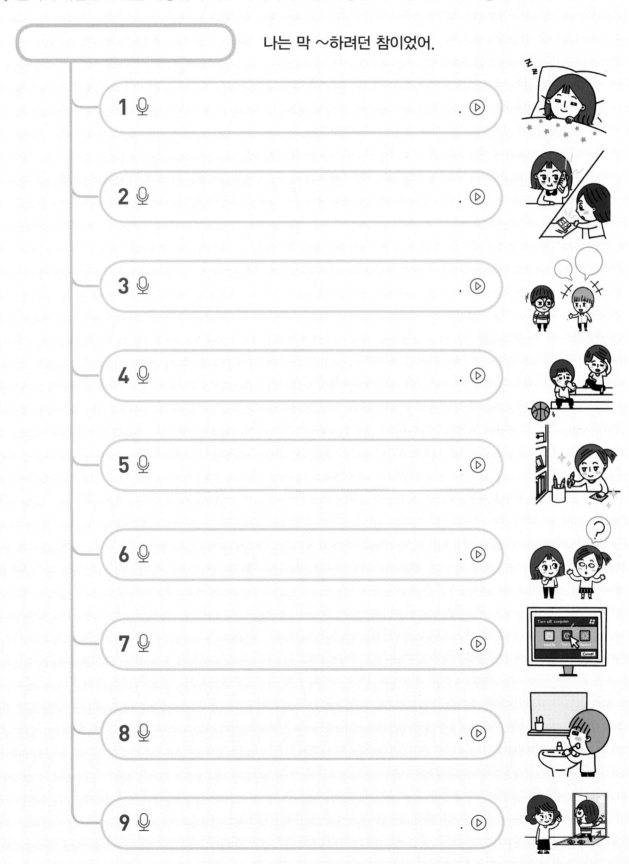

1 🎤 _____ .▷

2 🎤 _____ .▷

3 🎤 _____ .▷

4 🎤 _____ .▷

5 🎤 _____ .▷

6 🎤 _____ .▷

7 🎤 _____ .▷

8 🎤 _____ .▷

9 🎤 _____ .▷

53 Track

I'm going to school.

나는 ~하고 있어.

Master words & chunks!

A 상자 안에 있는 단어 조각들을 화살표로 연결하여 이번 트랙에서 배운 표현을 만들어 보세요.

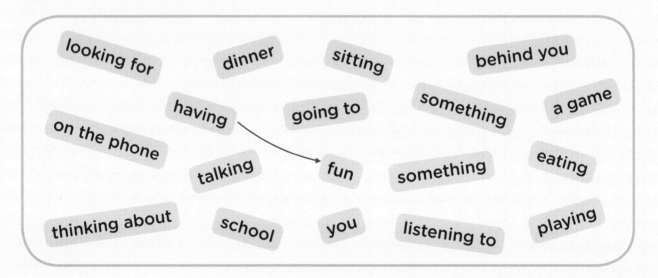

looking for　　dinner　　sitting　　behind you

having　　going to　　something　　a game

on the phone

talking　　fun　　something　　eating

thinking about　　school　　you　　listening to　　playing

B 상자에서 연결한 표현을 다시 한 번 써보고 뜻을 적어보세요.

Words & Chunks	뜻

Master sentences!

⭐ 앞에서 복습한 표현을 사용하여 이번 트랙에서 배운 문장을 각 그림에 맞게 완성해보세요.

나는 ~하고 있어.

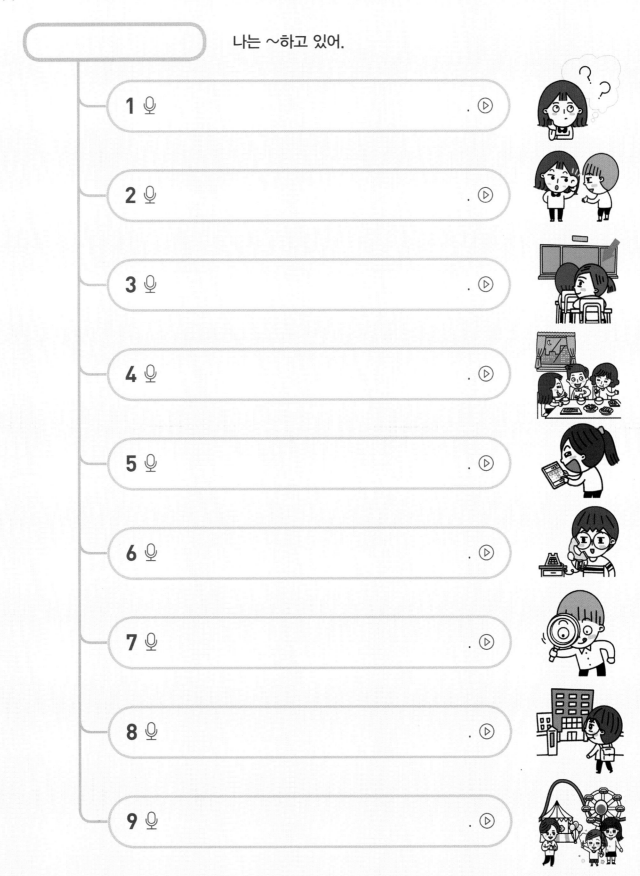

1 🎙 _____ . ▷

2 🎙 _____ . ▷

3 🎙 _____ . ▷

4 🎙 _____ . ▷

5 🎙 _____ . ▷

6 🎙 _____ . ▷

7 🎙 _____ . ▷

8 🎙 _____ . ▷

9 🎙 _____ . ▷

54
Track

He's eating lunch.

그[그녀]는 ~하고 있어.

Master words & chunks!

Ⓐ 상자 안에 있는 단어 조각들을 화살표로 연결하여 이번 트랙에서 배운 표현을 만들어 보세요.

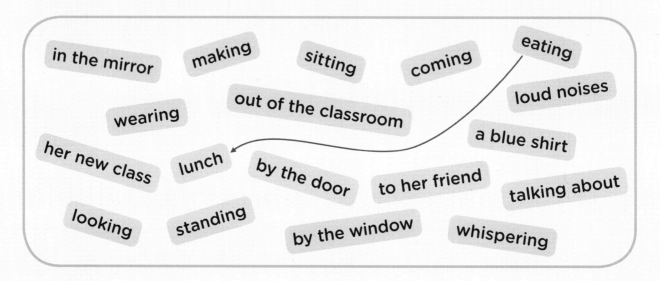

Ⓑ 상자에서 연결한 표현을 다시 한 번 써보고 뜻을 적어보세요.

Words & Chunks	뜻

Master sentences!

⭐ 앞에서 복습한 표현을 사용하여 이번 트랙에서 배운 문장을 각 그림에 맞게 완성해보세요.

그는 ~하고 있어.

1. 🎤 _____ . ▷

2. 🎤 _____ . ▷

3. 🎤 _____ . ▷

4. 🎤 _____ . ▷

그녀는 ~하고 있어.

5. 🎤 _____ . ▷

6. 🎤 _____ . ▷

7. 🎤 _____ . ▷

8. 🎤 _____ . ▷

9. 🎤 _____ . ▷

55

Track

Are you going home?

너는 ~하고 있어?

Master words & chunks!

Ⓐ 상자 안에 있는 단어 조각들을 화살표로 연결하여 이번 트랙에서 배운 표현을 만들어 보세요.

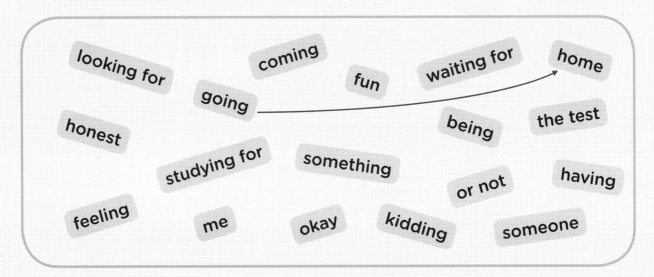

looking for　coming　fun　waiting for　home
going
honest　being　the test
studying for　something　having
feeling　me　okay　kidding　or not　someone

Ⓑ 상자에서 연결한 표현을 다시 한 번 써보고 뜻을 적어보세요.

Words & Chunks	뜻

Master sentences!

⭐ 앞에서 복습한 표현을 사용하여 이번 트랙에서 배운 문장을 각 그림에 맞게 완성해보세요.

너는 ~하고 있어?

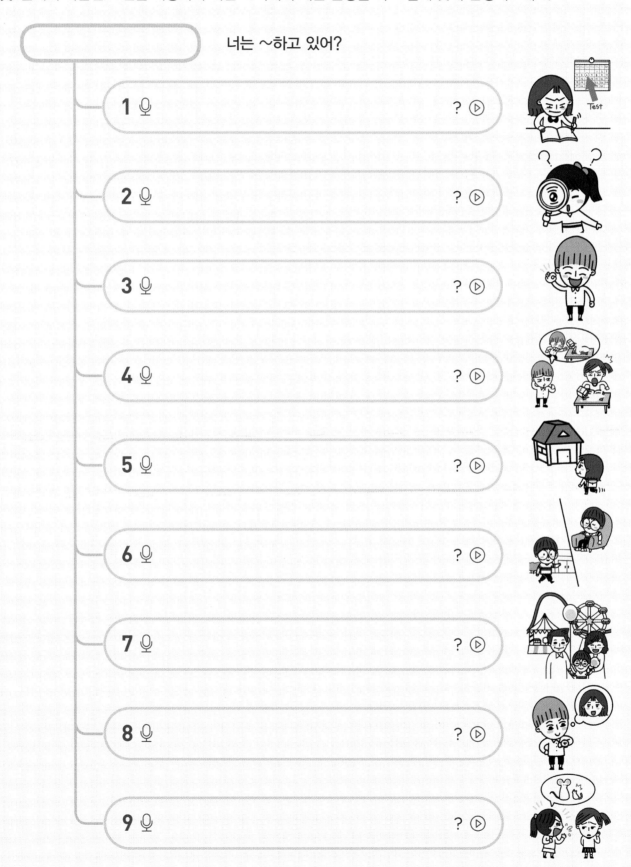

1 🎤   ? ▷

2 🎤   ? ▷

3 🎤   ? ▷

4 🎤   ? ▷

5 🎤   ? ▷

6 🎤   ? ▷

7 🎤   ? ▷

8 🎤   ? ▷

9 🎤   ? ▷

56 Track

I was helping my mom.

나는 ～하고 있었어.

Master words & chunks!

Ⓐ 상자 안에 있는 단어 조각들을 화살표로 연결하여 이번 트랙에서 배운 표현을 만들어 보세요.

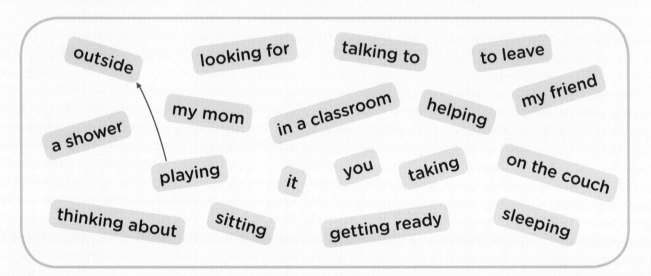

Ⓑ 상자에서 연결한 표현을 다시 한 번 써보고 뜻을 적어보세요.

Words & Chunks	뜻

Master sentences!

⭐ 앞에서 복습한 표현을 사용하여 이번 트랙에서 배운 문장을 각 그림에 맞게 완성해보세요.

나는 ~하고 있었어.

57
Track

What's your name?

~는 뭐야?

Master words & chunks!

⭐ 아래 적혀 있는 한글 뜻에 알맞은 단어를 상자 안에서 찾아 완성하고, 주어진 영어 표현에는
알맞은 한글 뜻을 쓰세요.

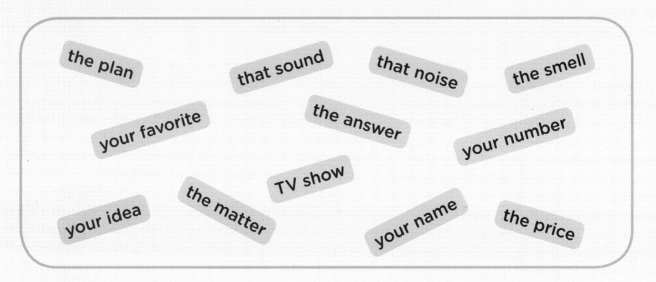

Words & Chunks	뜻
	너의 생각
	답
	계획
	저 시끄러운 소리
	네가 가장 좋아하는 TV 쇼
	(걱정·고민 등의 원인이 되는) 문제
the date	
	너의 이름
the lunch menu	

Master sentences!

앞에서 복습한 표현을 사용하여 이번 트랙에서 배운 문장을 각 그림에 맞게 완성해보세요.

~는 뭐야?

1 🎤   ? ▷

2 🎤   ? ▷

3 🎤   ? ▷

4 🎤   ? ▷

5 🎤   ? ▷

6 🎤   ? ▷

7 🎤   today? ▷

8 🎤   now? ▷

9 🎤   ? ▷

58 Track

What do you need?

너는 무엇을 ~하니(해)?

Master words & chunks!

A 상자 안에 있는 단어 조각들을 화살표로 연결하여 이번 트랙에서 배운 표현을 만들어 보세요.

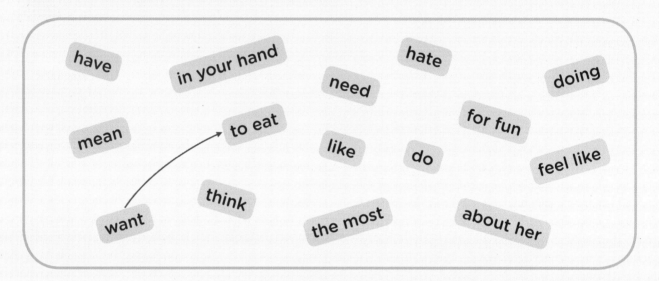

have   in your hand   hate   doing

need

mean   to eat   for fun

like   do   feel like

think

want   the most   about her

B 상자에서 연결한 표현과 남는 단어 조각을 다시 한 번 써보고 뜻을 적어보세요.

Words & Chunks	뜻

Master sentences!

⭐ 앞에서 복습한 표현을 사용하여 이번 트랙에서 배운 문장을 각 그림에 맞게 완성해보세요.

너는 무엇을 ～하니(해)?

1 🎤   ? ▷

2 🎤   ? ▷

3 🎤   ? ▷

4 🎤   ? ▷

5 🎤   ? ▷

6 🎤   ? ▷

7 🎤   ? ▷

8 🎤   ? ▷

9 🎤   ? ▷

59 Track

What are you **do**ing?

너는 무엇을 ~하고 있어?

Master words & chunks!

★ 아래 적혀 있는 한글 뜻에 알맞은 단어를 상자 안에서 찾아 완성하고, 주어진 영어 표현에는 알맞은 한글 뜻을 쓰세요.

waiting for	writing about	to do	thinking about
using	playing	looking for	laughing at
planning	looking at	making
talking about

Words & Chunks	뜻
	~에 대해 말하고 있는
eating	
	~을 기다리고 있는
doing	
	~을 보고 있는
	~에 대해 생각하고 있는
	~에 대해 웃고 있는
	~할 계획을 하고 있는
reading	

Master sentences!

★ 앞에서 복습한 표현을 사용하여 이번 트랙에서 배운 문장을 각 그림에 맞게 완성해보세요.

너는 무엇을 ～하고 있어?

1 🎤 ? ▶

2 🎤 ? ▶

3 🎤 ? ▶

4 🎤 ? ▶

5 🎤 ? ▶

6 🎤 ? ▶

7 🎤 ? ▶

8 🎤 tomorrow? ▶

9 🎤 ? ▶

Track 60

Who is your best friend?

~은 누구야?

Master words & chunks!

⭐ 아래 적혀 있는 한글 뜻에 알맞은 단어를 상자 안에서 찾아 완성하고, 주어진 영어 표현에는 알맞은 한글 뜻을 쓰세요.

your · with long hair · your · your · that boy · that girl · over there · this girl · in the picture · homeroom teacher · best friend · class president

Words & Chunks	뜻
	너의 가장 친한 친구
	너희 반장
	너희 담임 선생님
the boy next to you	
	저쪽에 있는 저 남자아이
	긴 머리를 가진 저 여자아이
	사진 속의 이 여자아이
the boy in the red T-shirt	

Master sentences!

⭐ 앞에서 복습한 표현을 사용하여 이번 트랙에서 배운 문장을 각 그림에 맞게 완성해보세요.

~은 누구야?

1 🎤 ? ▶

2 🎤 ? ▶

3 🎤 ? ▶

4 🎤 ? ▶

5 🎤 ? ▶

6 🎤 ? ▶

7 🎤 ? ▶

8 🎤 ? ▶

61 Track

Why do you say that?

너는 왜 ~해?

Master words & chunks!

A 상자 안에 있는 단어 조각들을 화살표로 연결하여 이번 트랙에서 배운 표현을 만들어 보세요.

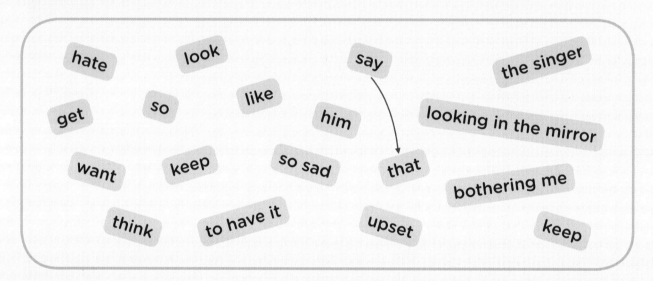

hate look say the singer

get so like him looking in the mirror

want keep so sad that bothering me

think to have it upset keep

B 상자에서 연결한 표현을 다시 한 번 써보고 뜻을 적어보세요.

Words & Chunks	뜻

Master sentences!

⭐ 앞에서 복습한 표현을 사용하여 이번 트랙에서 배운 문장을 각 그림에 맞게 완성해보세요.

너는 왜 ~해?

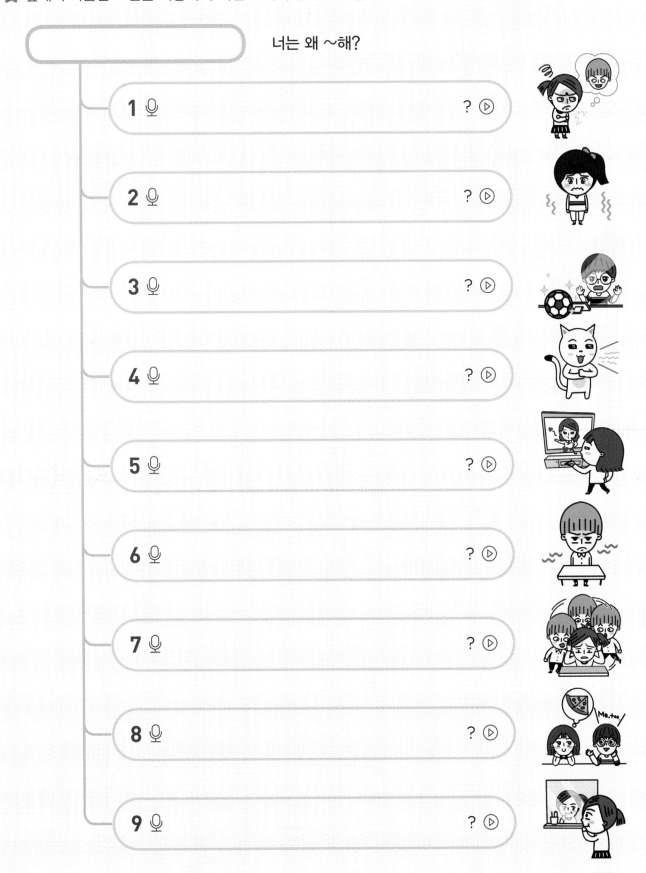

1 🎤   ? ▷

2 🎤   ? ▷

3 🎤   ? ▷

4 🎤   ? ▷

5 🎤   ? ▷

6 🎤   ? ▷

7 🎤   ? ▷

8 🎤   ? ▷

9 🎤   ? ▷

Why don't we go outside?

우리 ~하는 게 어때(~하지 않을래)?

Master words & chunks!

A 상자 안에 있는 단어 조각들을 화살표로 연결하여 이번 트랙에서 배운 표현을 만들어 보세요.

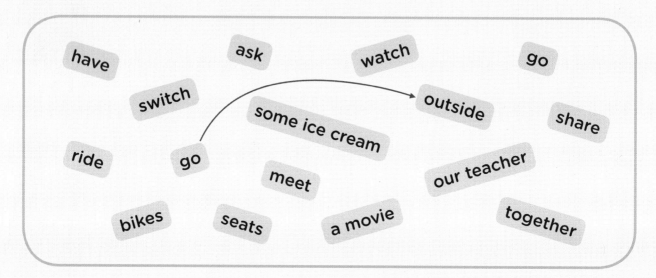

have   ask   watch   go

switch   outside   share

some ice cream

ride   go   our teacher

bikes   seats   meet   a movie   together

B 상자에서 연결한 표현과 남는 단어 조각을 다시 한 번 써보고 뜻을 적어보세요.

Words & Chunks	뜻

Master sentences!

★ 앞에서 복습한 표현을 사용하여 이번 트랙에서 배운 문장을 각 그림에 맞게 완성해보세요.

우리 ~하는 게 어때(~하지 않을래)?

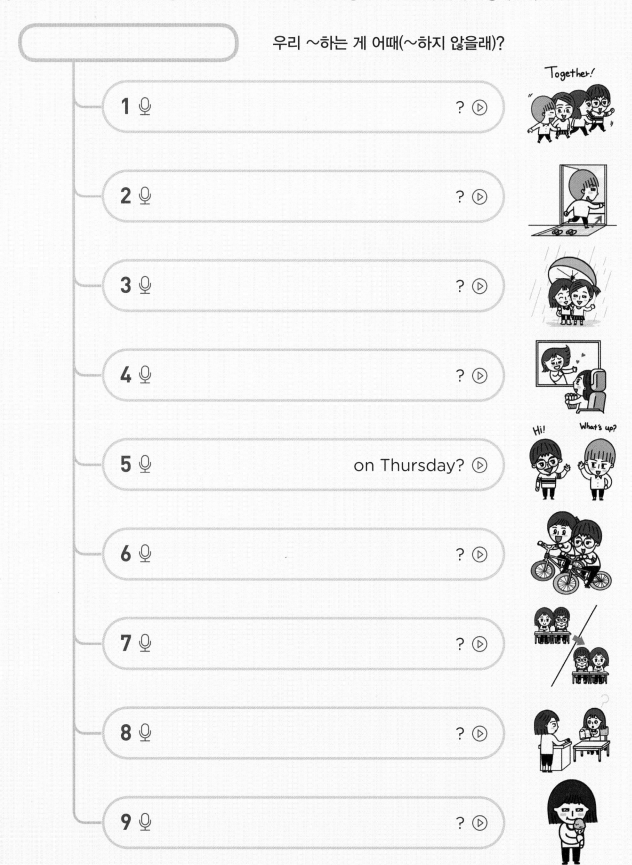

1 🎤 ? ▷

2 🎤 ? ▷

3 🎤 ? ▷

4 🎤 ? ▷

5 🎤 on Thursday? ▷

6 🎤 ? ▷

7 🎤 ? ▷

8 🎤 ? ▷

9 🎤 ? ▷

63 Track

Where is my umbrella?

~는 어디에 있어?

Master words & chunks!

⭐ 아래 적혀 있는 한글 뜻에 알맞은 단어를 상자 안에서 찾아 완성하고, 주어진 영어 표현에는 알맞은 한글 뜻을 쓰세요.

the bus stop   the bottle   the bathroom

my pencil

your house

my backpack   your school   my book

my umbrella   your sister   my green T-shirt

the cap

Words & Chunks	뜻
	너의 집
	내 책가방
	화장실
	내 초록색 티셔츠
	너의 학교
that grape juice	
	버스 정류장
	내 우산
Mom	

Master sentences!

⭐ 앞에서 복습한 표현을 사용하여 이번 트랙에서 배운 문장을 각 그림에 맞게 완성해보세요.

~는 어디에 있어?

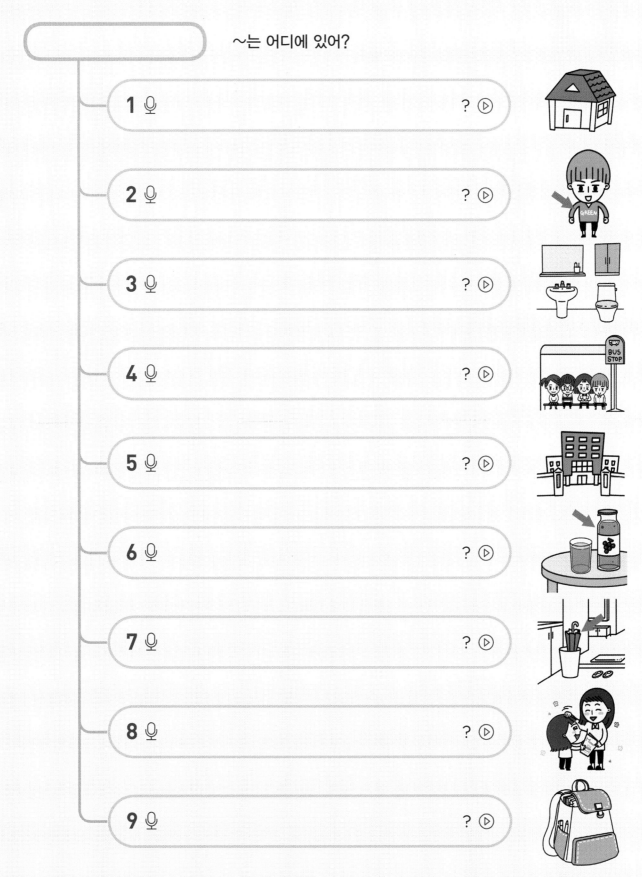

1 🎤   ? ▷

2 🎤   ? ▷

3 🎤   ? ▷

4 🎤   ? ▷

5 🎤   ? ▷

6 🎤   ? ▷

7 🎤   ? ▷

8 🎤   ? ▷

9 🎤   ? ▷

64
Track

Where did you buy it?

너는 어디에서 ~했어?

Master words & chunks!

Ⓐ 상자 안에 있는 단어 조각들을 화살표로 연결하여 이번 트랙에서 배운 표현을 만들어 보세요.

it
the ball
take
find
this picture
learn
for vacation
hear
it
buy
your umbrella
me
go
Taekwondo
put
see
lose
that

Ⓑ 상자에서 연결한 표현을 다시 한 번 써보고 뜻을 적어보세요.

Words & Chunks	뜻

Master sentences!

⭐ 앞에서 복습한 표현을 사용하여 이번 트랙에서 배운 문장을 각 그림에 맞게 완성해보세요.

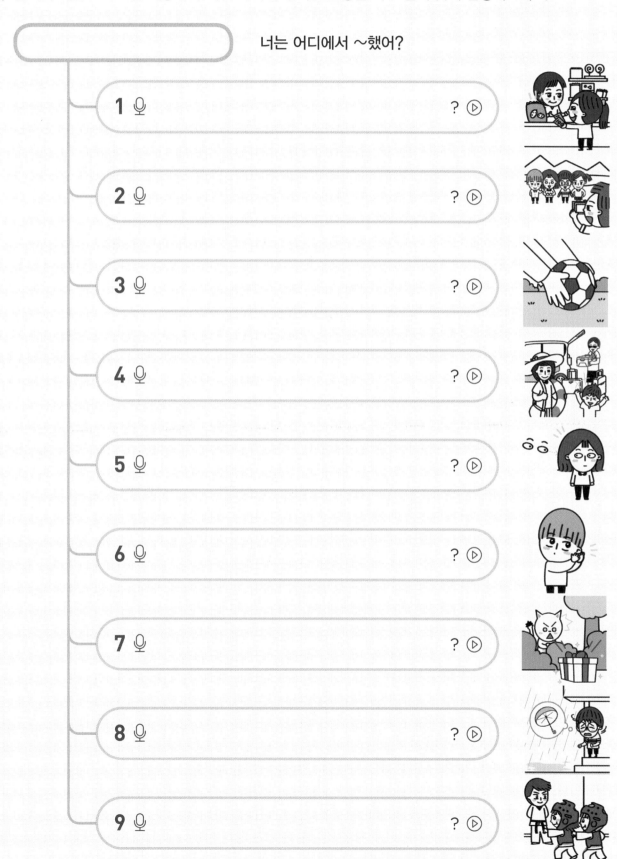

너는 어디에서 ~했어?

1 🎤   ? ▷

2 🎤   ? ▷

3 🎤   ? ▷

4 🎤   ? ▷

5 🎤   ? ▷

6 🎤   ? ▷

7 🎤   ? ▷

8 🎤   ? ▷

9 🎤   ? ▷

65
Track

How do you do that?
너는 어떻게 ~해?

Master words & chunks!

Ⓐ 상자 안에 있는 단어 조각들을 화살표로 연결하여 이번 트랙에서 배운 표현을 만들어 보세요.

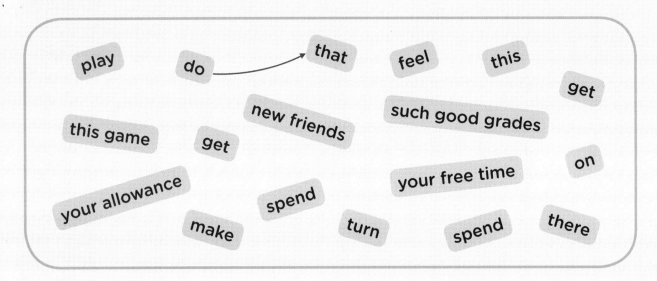

Ⓑ 상자에서 연결한 표현과 남는 단어 조각을 다시 한 번 써보고 뜻을 적어보세요.

Words & Chunks	뜻

Master sentences!

⭐ 앞에서 복습한 표현을 사용하여 이번 트랙에서 배운 문장을 각 그림에 맞게 완성해보세요.

너는 어떻게 ~해?

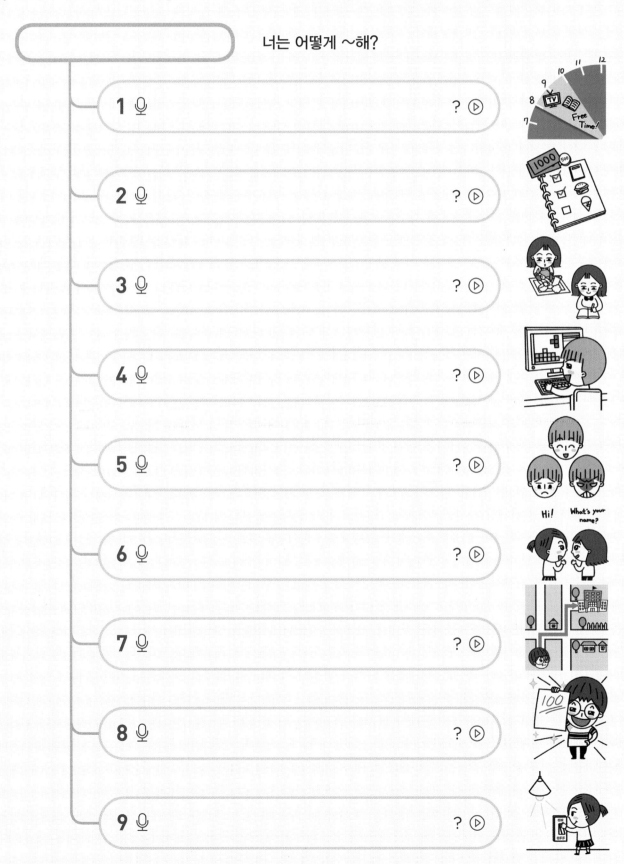

1 🎤 _____ ? ▷

2 🎤 _____ ? ▷

3 🎤 _____ ? ▷

4 🎤 _____ ? ▷

5 🎤 _____ ? ▷

6 🎤 _____ ? ▷

7 🎤 _____ ? ▷

8 🎤 _____ ? ▷

9 🎤 _____ ? ▷

66
Track

When are you going to come?

너는 언제 ~할 거야?

Master words & chunks!

Ⓐ 상자 안에 있는 단어 조각들을 화살표로 연결하여 이번 트랙에서 배운 표현을 만들어 보세요.

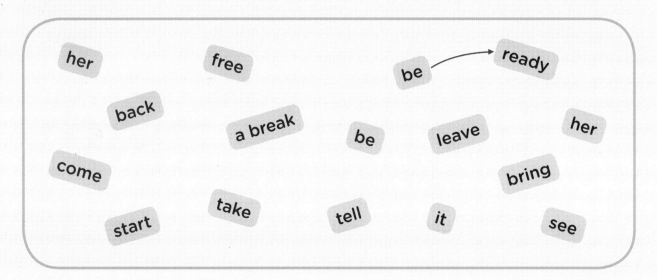

Ⓑ 상자에서 연결한 표현과 남는 단어 조각을 다시 한 번 써보고 뜻을 적어보세요.

Words & Chunks	뜻

Master sentences!

⭐ 앞에서 복습한 표현을 사용하여 이번 트랙에서 배운 문장을 각 그림에 맞게 완성해보세요.

너는 언제 ~할 거야?

1 🎤   ? ▷

2 🎤   ? ▷

3 🎤   ? ▷

4 🎤   ? ▷

5 🎤   ? ▷

6 🎤   ? ▷

7 🎤   ? ▷

8 🎤   ? ▷

9 🎤   ? ▷

67
Track

What a cool gift!

정말 ~이다(하다)!

Master words & chunks!

⭐ 아래 적혀 있는 한글 뜻에 알맞은 단어를 상자 안에서 찾아 완성하고, 주어진 영어 표현에는 알맞은 한글 뜻을 쓰세요.

a bad a mess cat a scary
to say
a cool a sad a poor
to think
a silly thing gift news

Words & Chunks	뜻
a great idea	
	불쌍한 고양이
	멋진 선물
a surprise	
	엉망진창
an amazing story	
a disappointment	
	어리석은 말

Master sentences!

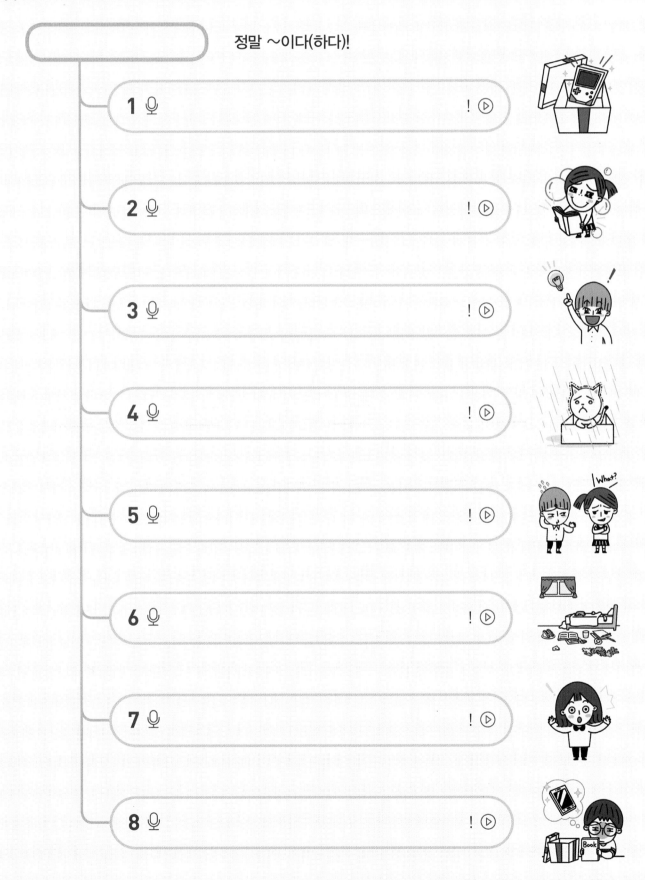

⭐ 앞에서 복습한 표현을 사용하여 이번 트랙에서 배운 문장을 각 그림에 맞게 완성해보세요.

정말 ～이다(하다)!

1 🎤   ! ▷

2 🎤   ! ▷

3 🎤   ! ▷

4 🎤   ! ▷

5 🎤   ! ▷

6 🎤   ! ▷

7 🎤   ! ▷

8 🎤   ! ▷

Be careful!

~해라(~해).

Master words & chunks!

Ⓐ 상자 안에 있는 단어 조각들을 화살표로 연결하여 이번 트랙에서 배운 표현을 만들어 보세요.

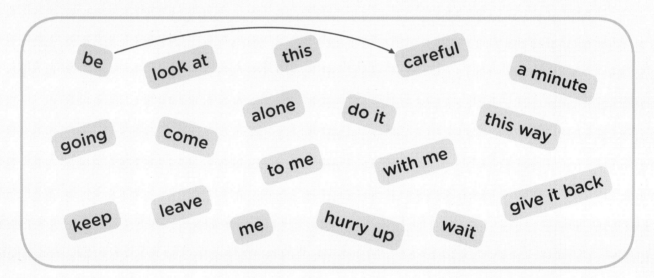

Ⓑ 상자에서 연결한 표현과 남는 단어 조각을 다시 한 번 써보고 뜻을 적어보세요.

Words & Chunks	뜻

Master sentences!

⭐ 앞에서 복습한 표현을 사용하여 이번 트랙에서 배운 문장을 각 그림에 맞게 완성해보세요.

~해라(~해).

1 🎙   ! ▷

2 🎙   . ▷

3 🎙   ! ▷

4 🎙   . ▷

5 🎙   ! ▷

6 🎙   . ▷

7 🎙   . ▷

8 🎙   . ▷

9 🎙   . ▷

Don't worry.

~하지 마.

Master words & chunks!

Ⓐ 상자 안에 있는 단어 조각들을 화살표로 연결하여 이번 트랙에서 배운 표현을 만들어 보세요.

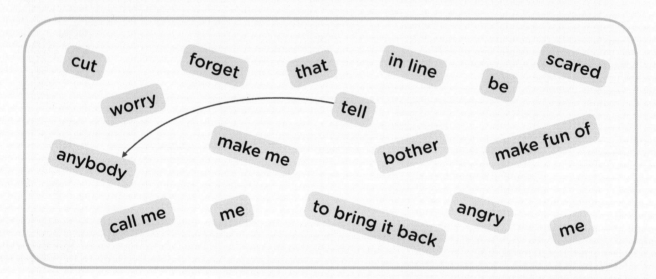

Ⓑ 상자에서 연결한 표현과 남는 단어 조각을 다시 한 번 써보고 뜻을 적어보세요.

Words & Chunks	뜻

Master sentences!

⭐ 앞에서 복습한 표현을 사용하여 이번 트랙에서 배운 문장을 각 그림에 맞게 완성해보세요.

~하지 마.

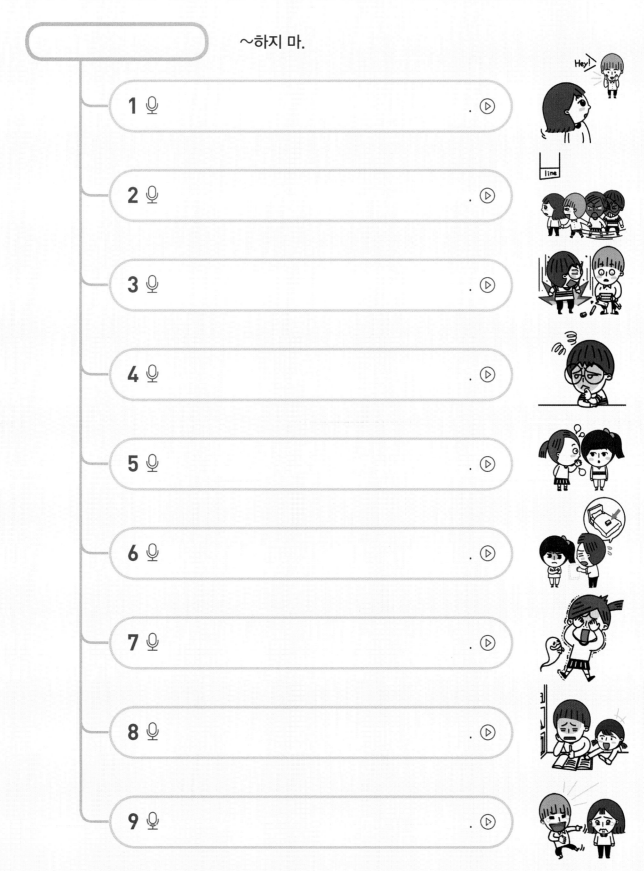

1 🎤   . ▷

2 🎤   . ▷

3 🎤   . ▷

4 🎤   . ▷

5 🎤   . ▷

6 🎤   . ▷

7 🎤   . ▷

8 🎤   . ▷

9 🎤   . ▷

70

Track

Let's meet at five.

~하자.

Master words & chunks!

Ⓐ 상자 안에 있는 단어 조각들을 화살표로 연결하여 이번 트랙에서 배운 표현을 만들어 보세요.

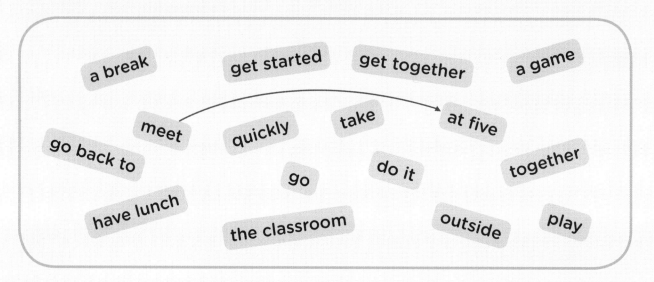

a break   get started   get together   a game

meet   quickly   take   at five

go back to   do it   together

go

have lunch   the classroom   outside   play

Ⓑ 상자에서 연결한 표현과 남는 단어 조각을 다시 한 번 써보고 뜻을 적어보세요.

Words & Chunks	뜻

Master sentences!

★ 앞에서 복습한 표현을 사용하여 이번 트랙에서 배운 문장을 각 그림에 맞게 완성해보세요.

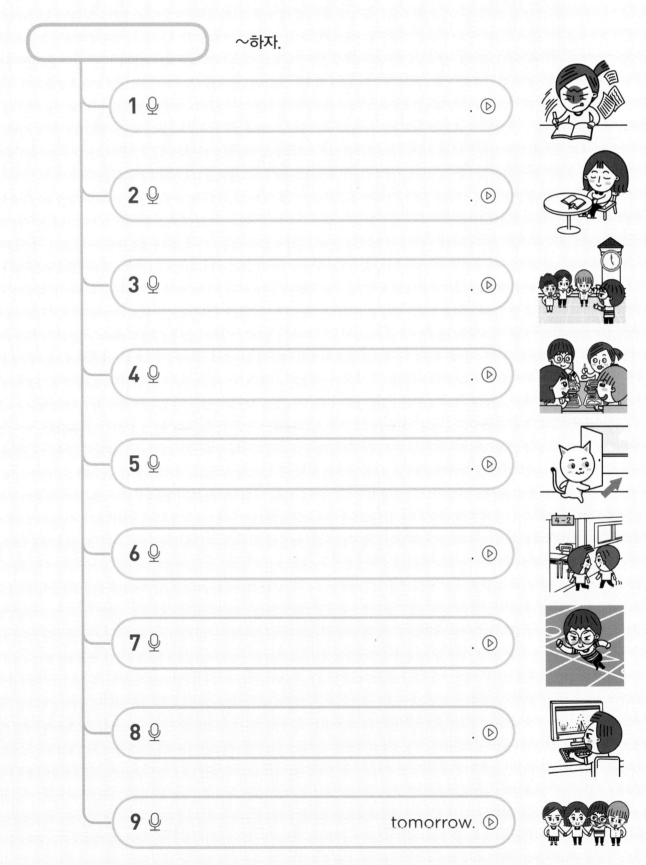

~하자.

1 🎤 _____ . ▷

2 🎤 _____ . ▷

3 🎤 _____ . ▷

4 🎤 _____ . ▷

5 🎤 _____ . ▷

6 🎤 _____ . ▷

7 🎤 _____ . ▷

8 🎤 _____ . ▷

9 🎤 _____ tomorrow. ▷

memo ✎

memo ✎

memo ✍

oh! my SPEAKING

오! 마이 스피킹

대상	예비 초 ~ 초등 4학년
구성	**Student Book**
	Workbook, MP3 CD, Picture Cards 포함

① 레벨 1 ~ 6으로 세분화된 레벨링

② 의사소통 중심의 수업을 위해
교사와 학생 모두에게 최적화된 구성

③ 전략적 반복 학습의 나선형 시스템

④ 말하기를 중심으로
어휘, 문법까지 통합적 학습 가능

오! 마이 스피킹 교재 특징

수준별 학습을 위한 6권 분류

1권 / 2권	Early Beginners
3권 / 4권	Beginners
5권 / 6권	Pre-Intermediates

세이펜 적용 도서

세이펜으로
원어민 발음을
학습하고, 혼자서도
재미있게 학습해요!

워크북 숙제도우미,
Christina(초코언니)

워크북 속 QR코드와
세이펜으로
Christina의 음성을
들을 수 있어요!

쎄듀북닷컴(www.cedubook.com)에서 부가 자료를 무료로 다운로드할 수 있습니다.

쎄듀

쎄듀 초등 커리큘럼

	예비초	초1	초2	초3	초4	초5	초6
구문				초등코치 천일문 SENTENCE 1001개 통문장 암기로 완성하는 초등 영어의 기초			
문법				초등코치 천일문 GRAMMAR 1001개 예문으로 배우는 초등 영문법			
			신간 왓츠 Grammar Start 시리즈 초등 기초 영문법 입문				
					신간 왓츠 Grammar Plus 시리즈 초등 필수 영문법 마무리		
독해					신간 왓츠 리딩 70 / 80 / 90 / 100 A / B 쉽고 재미있게 완성되는 영어 독해력		
어휘				초등코치 천일문 VOCA&STORY 1001개의 초등 필수 어휘와 짧은 스토리			
		패턴으로 말하는 초등 필수 영단어 1 / 2 문장 패턴으로 완성하는 초등 필수 영단어					
ELT	Oh! My PHONICS 1 / 2 / 3 / 4 유·초등학생을 위한 첫 영어 파닉스						
		Oh! My SPEAKING 1 / 2 / 3 / 4 / 5 / 6 핵심 문장 패턴으로 더욱 쉬운 영어 말하기					
		Oh! My GRAMMAR 1 / 2 / 3 쓰기로 완성하는 첫 초등 영문법					

쎄듀 중등 커리큘럼

	예비중	중1	중2	중3
구문		신간 천일문 STARTER 1 / 2		중등 필수 구문 & 문법 총정리
문법		천일문 GRAMMAR LEVEL 1 / 2 / 3		예문 중심 문법 기본서
		GRAMMAR Q Starter 1, 2 / Intermediate 1, 2 / Advanced 1, 2		학기별 문법 기본서
		잘 풀리는 영문법 1 / 2 / 3		문제 중심 문법 적용서
		GRAMMAR PIC 1 / 2 / 3 / 4		이해가 쉬운 도식화된 문법서
			1센치 영문법	1권으로 핵심 문법 정리
문법+어법			첫단추 BASIC 문법 · 어법편 1 / 2	문법 · 어법의 기초
문법+쓰기		EGU 영단어&품사 / 문장 형식 / 동사 써먹기 / 문법 써먹기 / 구문 써먹기		서술형 기초 세우기와 문법 다지기
				올씀 1 기본 문장 PATTERN 내신 서술형 기본 문장학습
쓰기		거침없이 Writing LEVEL 1 / 2 / 3		중등 교과서 내신 기출 서술형
		개정 중학 영어 쓰작 1 / 2 / 3		중등 교과서 패턴 드릴 서술형
어휘		어휘끝 중학 필수편 중학 필수어휘 1000개	어휘끝 중학 마스터편 고난도 중학어휘 +고등기초 어휘 1000개	
독해		Reading Relay Starter 1, 2 / Challenger 1, 2 / Master 1, 2		타교과 연계 배경 지식 독해
		READING Q Starter 1, 2 / Intermediate 1, 2 / Advanced 1, 2		예측/추론/요약 사고력 독해
독해전략		리딩 플랫폼 1 / 2 / 3		논픽션 지문 독해
독해유형		Reading 16 LEVEL 1 / 2 / 3		수능 유형 맛보기 + 내신 대비
			첫단추 BASIC 독해편 1 / 2	수능 유형 독해 입문
듣기	Listening Q 유형편 / 1 / 2 / 3			유형별 듣기 전략 및 실전 대비
		쎄듀 빠르게 중학영어듣기 모의고사 1 / 2 / 3		교육청 듣기평가 대비

Track | 49 I'm going to play outside.

p.14

p.14

Fill it!

A. 430   B. 437   C. 432   D. 435   E. 429
F. 433   G. 431   H. 436   I. 434

해석

429 나는 밖에서 놀 거야.
430 나는 친구들을 만날 거야.
431 나는 더 열심히 공부할 거야.
432 나는 할머니, 할아버지를 방문할 거야.
433 나는 샤워할 거야.
434 나는 창가에 앉을 거야.
435 나는 가족과 외식할 거야.
436 나는 수영하는 것을 배울 거야.
437 나는 내년에 4학년이 될 거야.

Study words & chunks!

429 play outside
430 meet my friends
431 study harder
432 visit my grandparents
433 take a shower
434 sit by the window
435 eat out with my family
436 learn to swim
437 be in fourth grade

Guess it!

1. I'm going to take a shower
2. I'm going to visit my grandparents
3. I'm going to play outside

Speak Up!

보기

A: 나 열심히 공부했는데 성적이 떨어졌어.
   나 슬퍼.
B: 힘내. 너는 다음번에 더 잘할 거야.
A: 고마워. **나는 더 열심히 공부할 거야.**

1. I'm going to eat out with my family(I'm going to meet my friends도 가능)
   A: 너 오늘 무슨 계획 있어?
   B: 응. **나는 가족과 외식할 거야[나는 친구들을 만날 거야].**
   A: 잘됐다. 너 어디로 갈 거야?

2. I'm going to learn to swim
   A: 너는 방학 동안 뭘 하고 싶어?
   B: **나는 수영하는 걸 배울 거야.** 나는 수영을 잘 하고 싶어.

3. I'm going to sit by the window
   A: **나는 창가에 앉을 거야.**
   B: 알겠어. 그런데 왜?
   A: 나는 차멀미를 하거든. 창가에서는 조금 나을 거야.

Track | 50 He's going to be fine.

p.18

p.18

Fill it!

A. 440   B. 444   C. 441   D. 443   E. 439
F. 438   G. 445   H. 442   I. 446

해석

438 그는 괜찮을 거야.
439 그는 그곳에 있을 거야.

440 그녀는 늦을 거야.
441 그녀는 나에게 전화할 거야.
442 그는 나를 도와줄 거야.
443 그녀는 그것을 정말 좋아할 거야.
444 그는 해낼 거야.
445 그녀는 놀랄 거야.
446 그녀는 반장이 될 거야.

Study words & chunks!

438 be fine 439 be there
440 be late 441 call me
442 help me 443 love it
444 make it
445 be surprised
446 be the class president

Guess it!

1. She's going to be the class president
2. She's going to be surprised
3. She's going to love it

Speak Up!

보기

A: 나는 제시간에 끝낼 수 있어.
B: 너 확실해? 그거 내일까지야.
A: 우리 오빠가 지금 집에 있어. **오빠가 나를 도와줄 거야.**

1. She's going to call me

A: 그 애는 어디에 있어?
B: 곧 올 거야. **그 애가 나한테 전화할 거야.**
A: 어! 네 전화가 울리고 있어. 분명 그 애일 거야.

2. He's going to be fine

A: 걱정하지 마. **그는 괜찮을 거야.**
B: 하지만 그 애는 괜찮아 보이지 않았어.
A: 그 애는 지금 보건실에서 쉬고 있어. 더 나아질 거야.

3. She's going to be late

A: 사라는 어디에 있어?
B: 사라가 나한테 메시지를 보냈어. **그녀는 늦을 거야.**
A: 알겠어. 안에서 기다리자.

Track | 51 Are you going to **say yes**? p.22

Fill it!

A. 454 B. 450 C. 453 D. 449 E. 455
F. 452 G. 451 H. 447 I. 448

해석

447 너는 여기에 앉을 거야?
448 너는 그것을 먹을 거야?
449 너는 그렇다고 말할 거야?
  (→너는 동의할[알겠다고 할] 거야?)
450 너는 무언가를 살 거야?
451 너는 엄마께 말씀드릴 거야?
452 너는 버스를 탈 거야?
453 너는 우리와 함께 갈 거야?
454 너는 나에게 화낼 거야?
455 너는 내 생일 파티에 올 거야?

Study words & chunks!

447 sit here 448 eat that
449 say yes 450 buy something
451 tell your mom
452 take the bus
453 come with us
454 be mad at me
455 come to my birthday party

Guess it!

1. Are you going to come with us
2. Are you going to take the bus
3. Are you going to buy something

Speak Up!

A: 댄이 우리 팀에 들어오고 싶다고 말했어.

B: 너 알겠다고 할 거야?

A: 잘 모르겠어. 그것에 대해 좀 얘기해보자.

1. Are you going to eat that

A: 너 그거 먹을 거야?

B: 아니, 나 배불러. 네가 먹어도 돼.

2. Are you going to tell your mom

A: 나 지갑을 잃어버린 것 같아.

B: 너 엄마께 말씀드릴 거야?

A: 이미 말씀드렸어. 지금 엄마가 여기로 오고 계셔.

3. Are you going to be mad at me

A: 너 대체 그 여자애한테 뭐라고 말한 거야? 말해봐!

B: 너 나한테 화낼 거야?

A: 하! 상황에 따라 다르겠지.

Track | 52   I was about to tell you.

p.26

Fill It!

A. 460   B. 462   C. 464   D. 459   E. 461
F. 458   G. 456   H. 463   I. 457

456 나는 막 너에게 전화하려던 참이었어.

457 나는 막 너에게 말하려던 참이었어.

458 나는 막 나가려던 참이었어.

459 나는 막 책상을 치우려던 참이었어.

460 나는 막 양치질을 하려던 참이었어.

461 나는 막 잠들려던 참이었어.

462 나는 막 잠깐 쉬려던 참이었어.

463 나는 막 너에게 무얼 물어보려던 참이었어.

464 나는 막 컴퓨터를 끄려던 참이었어.

Study words & chunks!

456 call you   457 tell you

458 go out

459 clean my desk

460 brush my teeth

461 fall asleep

462 take a break

463 ask you something

464 turn the computer off

Guess it!

1. I was about to turn the computer off

2. I was about to call you

3. I was about to clean my desk

Speak Up!

A: 너는 그것을 왜 비밀로 했어?

B: 미안해, 하지만 **나는 막 너에게 말하려던 참이었어.** 단지 너에게 말할 시간이 없었던 거야.

1. I was about to go out

A: 지금 비가 와. 근데 난 우산이 없어.

B: 나랑 같이 내 것 써도 돼. **나 막 나가려던 참이었어.**

2. I was about to fall asleep(I was about to take a break도 가능)

A: 야, 너 뭐 하고 있어?

B: 아, 너 왔구나. **나는 막 잠들려던 참이었어[나는 막 잠깐 쉬려던 참이었어].**

A: 정말? 나는 네가 열심히 공부하고 있다고 생각했어.

3. I was about to ask you something

A: 너 지금 가야 돼? **나는 막 너에게 뭐 좀 물어보려던 참이었어.**

B: 아니, 난 서두르지 않아도 돼. 뭔데?

A: 이 문제에 관한 거야. 난 도무지 이해가 안 돼.

Track | 53 　I'm going to school.

p.30

Fill it!

A. 465　B. 468　C. 467　D. 466　E. 473
F. 472　G. 471　H. 469　I. 470

해석

465　나는 재미있게 놀고 있어.
466　나는 저녁을 먹고 있어.
467　나는 학교에 가고 있어.
468　나는 네 말을 듣고 있어.
469　나는 게임을 하고 있어.
470　나는 네 뒤에 앉아 있어.
471　나는 전화 통화를 하고 있어.
472　나는 뭔가를 생각하고 있어.
473　나는 뭔가를 찾고 있어.

Study words & chunks!

465 having fun
466 eating dinner
467 going to school
468 listening to you
469 playing a game
470 sitting behind you
471 talking on the phone
472 thinking about something
473 looking for something

Guess it!

1. I'm talking on the phone
2. I'm having fun
3. I'm sitting behind you

Speak Up!

보기

A: 너 뭐 하고 있어?
B: 나는 게임을 하고 있어.
A: 재밌어 보인다. 게임 이름이 뭐야?

1. **I'm looking for something**
   A: 너 뭐 하고 있어?
   B: 나는 뭔가를 찾고 있어.
   A: 뭐가 필요한데? 내가 도와줄게.

2. **I'm listening to you**
   A: 내가 어제 어디 갔냐면... 야! 내가 지금 얘기
   　하고 있잖아.
   B: 나 네 말 듣고 있어. 계속 얘기해.

3. **I'm thinking about something**
   A: 너 왜 그렇게 심각해?
   B: 나는 뭔가를 생각하고 있어.
   A: 어떤 건데? 나한테 말해줄 수 있어?

Track | 54 　He's eating lunch.

p.34

Fill it!

A. 479　B. 482　C. 476　D. 478　E. 475
F. 481　G. 474　H. 477　I. 480

해석

474　그는 점심을 먹고 있어.
475　그녀는 파란색 셔츠를 입고 있어.
476　그는 시끄러운 소리를 내고 있어.
477　그녀는 문 옆에 서 있어.
478　그는 창가에 앉아 있어.
479　그녀는 거울을 보고 있어.
480　그는 교실 밖으로 나오고 있어.
481　그녀는 새로운 반에 대해 말하고 있어.
482　그녀는 친구에게 귓속말하고 있어.

Study words & chunks!

474 eating lunch
475 wearing a blue shirt
476 making loud noises

477 standing by the door
478 sitting by the window
479 looking in the mirror
480 coming out of the classroom
481 talking about her new class
482 whispering to her friend

Guess it!

1. She's whispering to her friend
2. She's looking in the mirror
3. She's standing by the door

Speak Up!

보기

A: 그가 어디 있지? 나 그 애한테 이걸 돌려
줘야 해.
B: 서기 봐! **그기 교실 밖으로 나오고 있어.**
A: 아, 저기 있네. 고마워.

1. He's making loud noises
   A: 그는 시끄러운 소리를 내고 있어. 뭘 하고 있
   는 거야?
   B: 그는 책상과 의자를 바깥으로 옮기고 있어.
   A: 정말 시끄럽다.

2. He's eating lunch
   A: 밖에 나가자.
   B: 하지만 우리는 테드를 기다려야 해. **그는 점
   심을 먹고 있어.**
   A: 아직도? 점심시간이 곧 끝날 거야.

3. He's sitting by the window
   A: 그 애 자리가 어디지? 그가 안 보이네.
   B: 그는 창가에 앉아 있어.
   A: 아, 찾았다.

Track | 55 Are you going home?

p.38

Fill it!

A. 488   B. 484   C. 491   D. 486   E. 490
F. 485   G. 487   H. 483   I. 489

해석

483 너는 집에 가고 있어?
484 너는 기분 괜찮아?
485 너는 재미있게 놀고 있어?
486 너는 솔직하게 하고 있어?
   (→너 사실대로 말하고 있는 거야?)
487 너 나한테 농담하고 있는 거야?
488 너는 오고 있어, 안 오고 있어?
489 너는 누군가를 기다리고 있어?
490 너는 시험공부 하고 있어?
491 너는 무언가를 찾고 있어?

Study words & chunks!

483 going home   484 feeling okay
485 having fun   486 being honest
487 kidding me

488 coming or not
489 waiting for someone
490 studying for the test
491 looking for something

Guess it!

1. Are you studying for the test
2. Are you feeling okay
3. Are you coming or not

Speak Up!

보기

A: 안녕. 너 어디 가는 중이야?
B: 나는 공원에 가고 있어. **너는 집에 가고
있어?**
A: 응. 나는 태권도 수업에서 집으로 가는
중이야.

1. Are you waiting for someone
   A: 너 여기서 뭐 하고 있어? **너 누구 기다리고
   있어?**

B: 응. 나는 여기서 내 친구를 만나기로 되어 있어.

2. Are you kidding me
(Are you being honest도 가능)
A: 너 이 사진 참 잘 나왔다.
B: 너 농담하는 거지[너 사실대로 말하고 있는 거야]? 나 눈 감았잖아!
A: 나는 그게 귀엽다고 생각해.

3. Are you looking for something
A: 너는 뭐 찾고 있어?
B: 응. 내가 공책을 가방에 넣어 놨는데 그게 안 보여.

Track | 56 I was helping my mom.

p.42

Fill it!
A. 497   B. 499   C. 498   D. 500   E. 495
F. 492   G. 494   H. 496   I. 493

해석
492 나는 밖에서 놀고 있었어.
493 나는 그것에 대해 생각하고 있었어.
494 나는 엄마를 돕고 있었어.
495 나는 샤워하고 있었어.
496 나는 너를 찾고 있었어.
497 나는 친구와 이야기하고 있었어.
498 나는 교실 안에 앉아 있었어.
499 나는 소파에서 자고 있었어.
500 나는 떠날 준비를 하고 있었어.

Study words & chunks!
492 playing outside
493 thinking about it
494 helping my mom
495 taking a shower
496 looking for you
497 talking to my friend
498 sitting in a classroom
499 sleeping on the couch
500 getting ready to leave

Guess it!
1. I was sleeping on the couch
2. I was getting ready to leave
3. I was sitting in a classroom

Speak Up!

보기
A: 어제 갑자기 비가 많이 왔어.
B: 응. 나는 밖에서 놀고 있었어. 비에 맞아서 다 젖어버렸어.

1. I was taking a shower
A: 너 왜 내 전화 안 받았어?
B: 나 욕실에 있었어. 땀을 많이 흘려서, 샤워하고 있었어.

2. I was helping my mom
A: 나 어제 너를 슈퍼마켓에서 봤어.
B: 정말? 나는 엄마를 도와드리고 있었어. 살 게 많았거든.

3. I was looking for you
A: 너 어디 있었어? 나는 너를 찾고 있었어.
B: 나 화장실 다녀왔어. 왜?

Track | 57   What's your name?

p.46

Fill it!

A. 502   B. 507   C. 509   D. 504   E. 501
F. 505   G. 503   H. 506   I. 508

해석

501 네 이름은 뭐야?

502 너의 생각은 뭐야? (→네 생각은 어때?)

503 답이 뭐야?

504 점심 메뉴는 뭐야?

505 지금 계획이 뭐야?

506 오늘 날짜가 뭐야? (→오늘 며칠이야?)

507 문제가 뭐야? (→무슨 일이야?)

508 저 시끄러운 소리는 뭐야?

509 네가 가장 좋아하는 TV 쇼는 뭐야?

Study words & chunks!

501 your name   **502** your idea

503 the answer

504 the lunch menu

505 the plan   **506** the date

507 the matter   **508** that noise

509 your favorite TV show

Guess it!

1. What's the answer

2. What's the lunch menu

3. What's your name

Speak Up!

보기

A: 나 그 애 선물 살 돈이 충분하지 않아.

B: 그래서 지금 **계획이 뭐야**?

A: 음, 그 애를 위해 뭔가를 만들 수 있을 것 같아.

1. **What's the date**
   A: 오늘 **며칠이야**?
   B: 7월 13일이야.
   A: 벌써? 우리 엄마 생신이 내일이야!

2. **What's that noise**
   A: **저 시끄러운 소리는 뭐야**?
   B: 위층에서 나는 거야.
   A: TV 소리가 안 들려. 소리가 너무 커.

3. **What's the matter**
   A: 안 돼!
   B: **무슨 일이야**?
   A: 내 자전거가 어디에서도 보이질 않아. 누군가가 훔쳐간 것 같아.

Track | 58   What do you need?

p.50

Fill it!

A. 514   B. 512   C. 518   D. 517   E. 513
F. 510   G. 511   H. 515   I. 516

해석

510 너는 무엇이 필요해?

511 너는 뭐라고 생각해[너는 어떤 것 같아]?

512 너는 무엇을 의미하니?
(→무슨 뜻이야?)

513 너는 재미를 위해 무엇을 하니?
(→너는 뭐 하고 놀아?)

514 너는 그녀의 무엇을 좋아해?
(→너는 그녀의 어떤 점을 좋아해?)

515 너는 손 안에 무엇을 가지고 있어?

516 너는 무엇을 가장 싫어해?

517 너는 뭐 먹고 싶어?

518 너는 뭐 하고 싶어?

Study words & chunks!

510 need   **511** think

512 mean   **513** do for fun

514 like about her

515 have in your hand

516 hate the most

517 want to eat

518 feel like doing

Guess it!

1. What do you like about her
2. What do you need
3. What do you have in your hand

Speak Up!

보기

A: 너 오늘 정말 달라 보여.

B: 무슨 뜻이야?

A: 너 보통 모자 안 쓰잖아. 그런데 너한테 잘 어울린다! 맘에 들어!

1. **What do you want to eat**

A: 너는 뭐 먹고 싶어?

B: 나는 치즈버거 먹을래. 너는 어때?

A: 나도 같은 거 먹을래.

2. **What do you hate the most**

A: 너는 무엇을 가장 싫어해?

B: 나는 거미를 정말 싫어해. 너는 어때?

A: 나도 역시 거미는 참을 수가 없어.

3. **What do you do for fun**

A: 너는 뭐 하고 놀아?

B: 나는 그림 그리는 것을 정말 좋아해.

A: 정말? 네 그림 봐도 돼?

Track | 59 What are you doing?   p.54

Fill it!

A. 521 B. 525 C. 527 D. 522 E. 519

F. 523 G. 526 H. 520 I. 524

해석

519 너는 뭐 하고 있어?

520 너는 뭐 먹고 있어?

521 너는 뭐 읽고 있어?

522 너는 뭐 보고 있어?

523 너는 뭐에 대해 말하고 있어?

(→너 무슨 말 하는 거야?)

524 너는 뭐에 대해 생각하고 있어?

(→너는 무슨 생각 하고 있어?)

525 너는 뭘 기다리고 있어?

526 너는 뭐에 대해 웃고 있어?

(→너는 뭐 때문에 웃고 있어?)

527 너는 내일 뭐 할 계획이야?

Study words & chunks!

519 doing   520 eating

521 reading   522 looking at

523 talking about

524 thinking about

525 waiting for   526 laughing at

527 planning to do

Guess it!

1. What are you laughing at
2. What are you eating
3. What are you reading

Speak Up!

보기

A: 우리 숙제 쉬웠어, 그렇지 않니?

B: 숙제? 너 무슨 말 하는 거야? 우리 숙제 있었어?

A: 응, 있었어! 너 잊어버린 거야?

1. **What are you doing**

A: 너 바빠 보인다. 뭐 하고 있어?

B: 나는 다음 수업을 위해 뭔가 만들고 있어.

A: 너 그거 지금 치워야 해. 수업이 곧 시작할 거야.

2. What are you looking at
A: 너 뭐 보고 있어?
B: 저쪽에 작은 강아지가 있어. 보여?
A: 응. 정말 귀엽다.

3. What are you planning to do
A: 야호! 내일은 공휴일이다!
B: 너는 내일 뭐 할 계획이야?
A: 나는 가족과 외식을 할 거야.

Track | 60 Who is your best friend?

Fill it!

A. 533   B. 528   C. 535   D. 532   E. 530
F. 531   G. 534   H. 529

해석

528 너의 가장 친한 친구는 누구야?
529 너희 반장은 누구야?
530 너희 담임 선생님은 누구셔?
531 네 옆에 있는 남자아이는 누구야?
532 저쪽에 있는 저 남자아이는 누구야?
533 긴 머리를 가진 저 여자아이는 누구야?
534 사진 속의 이 여자아이는 누구야?
535 빨간 티셔츠를 입은 남자아이는 누구야?

Study words & chunks!

528 your best friend
529 your class president
530 your homeroom teacher
531 the boy next to you
532 that boy over there
533 that girl with long hair
534 this girl in the picture
535 the boy in the red T-shirt

Guess it!

1. Who is that girl with long hair
2. Who is your homeroom teacher
3. Who is that boy over there

Speak Up!

보기

A: 나 놀이공원에서 사진 찍었어!
B: 내가 좀 볼게. 사진 속의 이 여자아이는 누구야?
A: 아, 그 애는 내 여동생이야.

1. Who is the boy in the red T-shirt
A: 빨간 티셔츠를 입은 남자아이는 누구야?
B: 그 애는 내 남동생이야. 그 색은 그 애가 제일 좋아하는 색이야.
A: 그런 것 같아. 빨간색 신발도 신고 있네!

2. Who is your class president
A: 너희 반장은 누구야?
B: 문 옆에 있는 저 남자애야. 그 애가 가장 많은 표를 받았어.

3. Who is your best friend
A: 나는 나의 가장 친한 친구한테 편지를 쓰고 있어.
B: 너의 가장 친한 친구가 누구야?
A: 그 애의 이름은 루시야. 그 애는 5반이야.

Track | 61 Why do you say that?

p.62

Fill it!

A. 542   B. 538   C. 541   D. 540   E. 544
F. 539   G. 537   H. 543   I. 536

해석

536 너는 왜 그것을 말해?
      (→너는 왜 그런 말을 해?)
537 너는 왜 그 가수를 좋아해?
538 너는 왜 그를 싫어해?
539 너는 왜 그렇게 생각해?
540 너는 왜 매우 슬퍼 보여?
      (→너는 왜 그렇게 슬퍼 보여?)
541 너는 왜 속상해해?
542 너는 왜 그것을 가지고 싶어?
543 너는 왜 거울을 계속 들여다봐?
544 너는 왜 나를 계속 귀찮게 해?

Study words & chunks!

536 say that   537 like the singer
538 hate him   539 think so
540 look so sad   541 get upset
542 want to have it
543 keep looking in the mirror
544 keep bothering me

Guess it!

1. Why do you keep bothering me
2. Why do you like the singer
3. Why do you hate him

Speak Up!

보기

A: 곧 비가 올 것 같아.
B: 왜 그렇게 생각해?
A: 어두워지기 시작하고 있잖아. 날씨도 매우 흐려.

1. Why do you keep looking in the mirror
   A: 너는 왜 거울을 계속 들여다봐?
   B: 내 앞머리 확인하고 있어. 앞머리가 너무 짧은 것 같아.
   A: 걱정하지 마. 네 앞머리는 괜찮아.

2. Why do you look so sad
   A: 너는 왜 그렇게 슬퍼 보여?
   B: 우리 집 개가 정말 아파서 지금 병원에 있거든.
   A: 그것 참 안됐다.

3. Why do you want to have it
   A: 나는 내 생일에 이 만화책을 가지고 싶어.
   B: 그걸 왜 가지고 싶어?
   A: 그건 내가 가장 좋아하는 만화책 시리즈의 마지막 책이거든.

Track | 62 Why don't we go outside?

p.66

Fill it!

A. 549   B. 545   C. 548   D. 552   E. 546
F. 550   G. 551   H. 547   I. 553

해석

545 우리 밖으로 나가는 게 어때?
546 우리 같이 가는 게 어때?
547 우리 같이 쓰는 게 어때?
548 우리 자전거 타는 게 어때?
549 우리 영화 보는 게 어때?
550 우리 선생님께 여쭤보는 게 어때?
551 우리 아이스크림 먹는 게 어때?
552 우리 자리를 바꾸는 게 어때?
553 우리 목요일에 만나는 게 어때?

Study words & chunks!

545 go outside   546 go together

547 share   548 ride bikes
549 watch a movie
550 ask our teacher
551 have some ice cream
552 switch seats   553 meet

Guess it!

1. Why don't we have some ice cream
2. Why don't we watch a movie
3. Why don't we share

Speak Up!

보기

A: 우리 목요일에 **만나는 게 어때?**
B: 나는 그날 다른 계획이 있어. 금요일은 어때?
A: 그래.

1. **Why don't we switch seats**
   A: 너 안 좋아 보여. 무슨 일이야?
   B: 나 속이 안 좋아. 나는 버스에서 항상 속이 안 좋아지거든.
   A: **우리 자리를 바꾸는 게 어때?** 그게 도움이 될 수 있어.

2. **Why don't we ride bikes**
   A: **우리 자전거 타는 게 어때?**
   B: 그러고 싶은데, 나는 그럴 수 없어. 나는 자전거가 없거든.
   A: 내가 두 대 있어. 너는 내 것 중에 하나 타도 돼.

3. **Why don't we ask our teacher**
   A: 그 애 오늘 결석했어. 그 애에게 무슨 일 있었나?
   B: 나도 모르겠어. **우리 선생님께 여쭤보는 게 어때?**
   A: 그래.

Track | 63 Where is my umbrella?

p.70

Fill it!

A. 560   B. 561   C. 554   D. 556   E. 558
F. 557   G. 555   H. 562   I. 559

해석

554 엄마는 어디에 계셔?
555 너의 학교는 어디에 있어?
556 너의 집은 어디에 있어?
557 내 우산은 어디에 있어?
558 내 책가방은 어디에 있어?
559 내 초록색 티셔츠는 어디에 있어?
560 그 포도 주스는 어디에 있어?
561 화장실은 어디에 있어?
562 버스 정류장은 어디에 있어?

Study words & chunks!

554 Mom   555 your school
556 your house   557 my umbrella
558 my backpack
559 my green T-shirt

560 that grape juice
561 the bathroom
562 the bus stop

Guess it!

1. Where is the bathroom
2. Where is my green T-shirt
3. Where is my backpack

Speak Up!

보기

A: **내 우산은 어디에 있지?**
B: 너 문 옆에 있는 통 확인했어?
A: 했는데, 거기에 없어. 나 다 젖겠다.

1. **Where is Mom**
   A: 엄마는 어디에 계셔?
   B: 시장에 가셨어. 엄마는 곧 돌아오실 거야.

2. **Where is that grape juice**
   A: 그 포도 주스 어디에 있어?

B: 미안해, 내가 다 마셨어.

A: 아, 그러면 난 그 대신에 그냥 물을 마실게.

3. Where is your house

A: 나 새로운 게임 샀어. 너 와서 게임할래?

B: 물론이지. **너의 집은 어디인데?**

A: 우리 학교에 아주 가까이 있어.

Track | 64 Where did you buy it?   p.74

Fill it!

A. 564   B. 567   C. 563   D. 570   E. 571
F. 566   G. 569   H. 565   I. 568

> **해석**
>
> **563** 너는 어디에서 나를 봤어?
>
> **564** 너는 어디에서 그것을 샀어?
>
> **565** 너는 어디에서 그것을 찾았어?
>
> **566** 너는 어디에 공을 놓았어?
>
> **567** 너는 어디에서 태권도를 배웠어?
>
> **568** 너는 어디에서 그것을 들었어?
>
> **569** 너는 어디로 휴가를 갔어?
>
> **570** 너는 어디에서 이 사진을 찍었어?
>
> **571** 너는 어디에서 우산을 잃어버렸어?

Study words & chunks!

563 see me   564 buy it

565 find it   566 put the ball

567 learn Taekwondo

568 hear that

569 go for vacation

570 take this picture

571 lose your umbrella

Guess it!

1. Where did you go for vacation
2. Where did you put the ball
3. Where did you lose your umbrella

Speak Up!

> **보기**
>
> **A:** 네 필통 맘에 들어. **너 그거 어디에서 샀어?**
>
> **B:** 이모가 사 주셨어. 선물이야.

1. Where did you hear that

A: 오늘 우리 일찍 갈 수 있어!

B: 확실해? **너 그거 어디서 들었어?**

A: 선생님이 아침에 말씀해 주셨어.

2. Where did you take this picture

A: **너 이 사진 어디서 찍었어?** 바다색이 아주 멋져!

B: 제주도에서 찍었어. 가족과 함께 다녀왔어.

3. Where did you learn Taekwondo

A: **너 태권도 어디에서 배웠어?**

B: 나 방과 후 수업 들었어. 진짜 재밌었어!

Track | 65 How do you do that?   p.78

Fill it!

A. 577   B. 579   C. 576   D. 575   E. 580
F. 572   G. 574   H. 578   I. 573

> **해석**
>
> **572** 너는 기분이 어때[너 몸 상태는 어때]?

573 너는 그것을 어떻게 해?

574 너는 그곳에 어떻게 가?

575 너는 이 게임을 어떻게 해?

576 너는 새로운 친구들을 어떻게 사귀어?

577 너는 이것을 어떻게 켜?

578 너는 어떻게 그렇게 좋은 성적을 받아?

579 너는 자유 시간을 어떻게 보내?
580 너는 용돈을 어떻게 써?

Study words & chunks!

572 feel   573 do that
574 get there
575 play this game
576 make new friends
577 turn this on
578 get such good grades
579 spend your free time
580 spend your allowance

Guess it!

1. How do you get such good grades
2. How do you do that
3. How do you turn this on

Speak Up!

A: 그거 새로운 게임이야?
B: 응. 이거 쉽고 재밌어. 여기, 너 해 봐도 돼.
A: 이 게임 어떻게 해?

1. How do you feel
A: 너 몸 상태는 어때?
B: 나 이제 나아졌어. 어제 병원에 갔었거든.
A: 잘됐다.

2. How do you spend your free time
A: 너는 자유 시간을 어떻게 보내?
B: 나는 보통 게임을 해. 너는 어때?
A: 나는 가족과 TV 보는 것을 즐겨.

3. How do you make new friends
A: 너는 새 친구를 어떻게 사귀어?
B: 나는 항상 먼저 인사해. 그리고 나는 그 애들이 가장 좋아하는 물건에 관심을 보여.
A: 아, 그거 좋다. 나도 그렇게 해 봐야지.

Track | 66   When are you going to come?   p.82

Fill it!

A. 584   B. 582   C. 585   D. 586   E. 587
F. 583   G. 581   H. 589   I. 588

해석
581 너는 언제 올 거야?
582 너는 언제 시작할 거야?
583 너는 언제 준비될 거야?
    (→너는 언제 준비될 것 같아?)
584 너는 언제 그녀를 만날 거야?
585 너는 언제 그녀에게 말할 거야?
586 너는 언제 시간이 나?
587 너는 언제 잠시 쉴 거야?
588 너는 언제 출발할 거야?
589 너는 언제 그것을 돌려줄 거야?

Study words & chunks!

581 come   582 start
583 be ready   584 see her
585 tell her   586 be free

587 take a break   588 leave
589 bring it back

Guess it!

1. When are you going to bring it back
2. When are you going to leave
3. When are you going to see her

Speak Up!

보기
A: 우리 지금 그것에 대해 얘기할 수 있어?
B: 미안한데, 나 이거 먼저 끝내야 해.
A: 너는 언제 시간이 나? 그때 내가 너한테 전화할게.

1. When are you going to tell her
A: 너 엄마께 깨진 창문에 대해 말씀드렸어?
B: 아직 안 했어. 나 무서워.
A: 언제 엄마께 말씀드릴 거야? 얼른 해야 해.

2. When are you going to be ready
   A: 너 언제 준비될 것 같아? 우리 서둘러야 해.
   B: 준비 거의 다 됐어. 잠깐만 시간을 줘.

3. When are you going to start
   A: 나 기타 수업받을 거야.
   B: 멋지다. **언제 시작할 거야?**
   A: 다음 달에. 정말 신나.

Track | 67　What a cool gift!
p.86

Fill it!
A. 593　B. 590　C. 597　D. 596　E. 594
F. 592　G. 595　H. 591

> **해석**
>
> **590** 정말 훌륭한 생각이다!
> **591** 정말 불쌍한 고양이다!
> **592** 정말 멋진 선물이다!
> **593** 정말 놀라운 일이다! (→정말 놀랍다!)
> **594** 정말 엉망진창이야!
> **595** 정말 굉장한 이야기다!
> **596** 정말 실망스럽다!
> **597** 정말 어리석은 말이다!

Study words & chunks!
590 a great idea　　591 a poor cat
592 a cool gift　　　593 a surprise
594 a mess
595 an amazing story
596 a disappointment
597 a silly thing to say

Guess it!
1. What a surprise
2. What a poor cat
3. What a cool gift

Speak Up!

> **보기**
>
> **A:** 우리 방학 동안 숙제가 정말 많아.
> **B:** **정말 실망스럽다!** 너 그거 다 할 수 있어?
> **A:** 잘 모르겠어. 그래도 노력할 거야.

1. What a mess
   A: **정말 엉망진창이야!** 모든 곳에 물건들이 있어!
   B: 맞아. 내가 금방 치울 거야.
   A: 엄마가 곧 집에 오실 거야. 너 지금 해야 돼.

2. What a great idea
   A: 그 애의 생일이 다가오고 있어.
   B: 응, 그러네. 우리 선물로 그 애를 놀라게 해 주는 게 어때?
   A: **정말 훌륭한 생각이다!** 계획을 세우자.

3. What an amazing story
   A: 너 그 책 읽는 거 다 끝났어?
   B: 응! **정말 굉장한 이야기야!**
   A: 맞아. 나는 빨리 페이지를 넘기고 싶었어.

Track | 68　Be careful!
p.90

Fill it!
A. 601　B. 606　C. 599　D. 604　E. 602
F. 605　G. 603　H. 600　I. 598

> **해석**
>
> **598** 서둘러!
> **599** 조심해!
> **600** 이것 좀 봐!

601 잠깐만 기다려.
602 그건 이렇게 해.
603 나랑 같이 가.
604 나한테 그것을 돌려줘.
605 나를 혼자 내버려 둬.
606 계속해[계속 가].

Study words & chunks!

598 Hurry up   599 Be careful
600 Look at this
601 Wait a minute
602 Do it this way
603 Come with me
604 Give it back to me
605 Leave me alone
606 Keep going

Guess it!

1. Be careful
2. Come with me
3. Look at this

Speak Up!

보기
A: 너 이게 맞는 길인지 확실해? 나는 헷갈려.
B: 응. **계속 가**. 우리 거의 다 왔어.

1. Wait a minute
A: 나 너의 집에 가도 돼?
B: 내가 엄마한테 먼저 여쭤볼게. **잠깐만 기다려.**
A: 알겠어.

2. Hurry up
A: 너 나갈 준비 됐어?
B: 아니. 나 옷 갈아입어야 해.
A: **서둘러!** 우리는 시간이 충분하지 않아.

3. Give it back to me
A: 그거 내 일기장이잖아! 네가 이걸 왜 가지고 있어?
B: 난 그냥 이것을 주웠을 뿐이야.
A: **나한테 그거 돌려줘**. 너 그거 읽었어?

Track | 69 Don't worry.

p.94

Fill it!

A. 611   B. 608   C. 614   D. 615   E. 607
F. 609   G. 612   H. 613   I. 610

해석
607 걱정하지 마.
608 아무한테도 말하지 마.
609 나를 그렇게 부르지 마.
610 나를 귀찮게 하지 마.
611 무서워하지 마.
612 새치기하지 마.
613 나를 화나게 하지 마.
614 나를 놀리지 마.
615 그것을 돌려주는 걸 잊지 마.

609 call me that   610 bother me
611 be scared   612 cut in line
613 make me angry
614 make fun of me
615 forget to bring it back

Guess it!

1. Don't worry
2. Don't tell anybody
3. Don't bother me

Speak Up!

보기
A: 너희 개 정말 크다.
B: **무서워하지 마.** 우리 개는 안 물어.
A: 나는 무섭지 않아. 그냥 조금 놀랐을 뿐이야.

Study words & chunks!

607 worry   608 tell anybody

1. Don't cut in line

A: 줄에 사람들이 너무 많이 있어.

B: 어, 앞에 내 친구가 보인다. 우리 그 애 뒤에 설 수 있을지도 몰라.

A: 새치기하지 마. 그건 공평하지 않아.

2. don't forget to bring it back

A: 네 미술책 좀 빌릴 수 있을까?

B: 물론이지. 근데 **그것을 돌려주는 걸 잊지 마.** 나 내일 필요하거든.

3. Don't make fun of me

A: 나 네가 얼음 위에서 미끄러졌을 때 봤어. 웃기더라.

B: 나 놀리지 마. 정말 아팠단 말이야.

Track | 70 Let's meet at five.   p.98

Fill it!

A. 622   B. 617   C. 616   D. 618   E. 621
F. 624   G. 619   H. 623   I. 620

> **해석**
>
> 616 밖으로 나가자.
> 617 게임하자.
> 618 다섯 시에 만나자.
> 619 잠시 쉬자.
> 620 그것을 빨리하자.
> 621 점심 같이 먹자.
> 622 시작하자.
> 623 내일 모이자.
> 624 교실로 돌아가자.

Study words & chunks!

616 go outside   617 play a game
618 meet at five   619 take a break
620 do it quickly
621 have lunch together
622 get started   623 get together
624 go back to the classroom

Guess it!

1. Let's take a break
2. Let's go outside
3. Let's get started

Speak Up!

> **보기**
>
> **A:** 우리 모둠 숙제 시작해야 해.
> **B:** 나중에 하면 안 될까? 나는 지금 하고 싶지 않아.
> **A:** 어서! **빨리하자.** 그다음에 놀면 돼.

1. Let's play a game

A: 나 너무 지루해. 뭐 재밌는 거 없어?

B: 게임하자.

A: 좋아! 어떤 게임이야?

2. Let's meet at five

A: 그 애가 생일 파티에 너 초대했어?

B: 응. 그런데 나 거기에 가는 방법을 몰라.

A: 우리 같이 가면 돼. **다섯 시에 만나자.**

3. Let's go back to the classroom

A: 얼른 와. 수업이 막 시작하려고 해.

B: 하지만 나 화장실에 가고 싶어.

A: 시간이 별로 없어. **교실로 돌아가자.**

초 등 코 치

천일문
sentence

✦ ✦ ✦

WORKBOOK
정답과 해설

3

Track 49 p.2

Master words & chunks!

(순서 상관없음)

play outside, 밖에서 놀다
meet my friends, 내 친구들을 만나다
study harder, 더 열심히 공부하다
visit my grandparents, 나의 할머니, 할아
버지를 방문하다
take a shower, 샤워하다
sit by the window, 창가에 앉다
eat out with my family, 나의 가족과 외식
하다
learn to swim, 수영하는 것을 배우다
be in fourth grade, 4학년이 되다

Master sentences!

[I'm going to]

1 visit my grandparents
2 play outside
3 sit by the window
4 study harder
5 meet my friends
6 be in fourth grade
7 take a shower
8 eat out with my family
9 learn to swim

Track 50 p.4

Master words & chunks!

(순서 상관없음)

be fine, 괜찮다
be there, 그곳에 있다
be late, 늦다
call me, 나에게 전화하다
help me, 나를 도와주다
love it, 그것을 정말 좋아하다
make it, 해내다
be surprised, 놀라다
be the class president, 반장이 되다

Master sentences!

[He's going to]

1 make it
2 be fine
3 help me
4 be there

[She's going to]

5 love it
6 be late
7 be surprised
8 call me
9 be the class president

Track 51 p.6

Master words & chunks!

(순서 상관없음)

sit here, 여기에 앉다
eat that, 그것을 먹다
say yes, 그렇다고 말하다
buy something, 무언가를 사다
tell your mom, 너의 엄마께 말씀드리다
take the bus, 버스를 타다
come with us, 우리와 함께 가다
be mad at me, 나에게 화가 나다
come to my birthday party, 내 생일 파
티에 오다

Master sentences!

[Are you going to]

1 come with us
2 tell your mom
3 sit here
4 take the bus
5 buy something
6 be mad at me
7 come to my birthday party
8 eat that
9 say yes

Track 52 p.8

Master words & chunks!

(순서 상관없음)

call you, 너에게 전화하다

tell you, 너에게 말하다

go out, 나가다, 외출하다

clean my desk, 내 책상을 치우다

brush my teeth, 양치질하다

fall asleep, 잠들다

take a break, 잠시 쉬다

ask you something, 너에게 무언가를 물어
보다

turn the computer off[turn off the
computer], 컴퓨터를 끄다

Master sentences!

I was about to

1 fall asleep

2 call you

3 tell you

4 take a break

5 clean my desk

6 ask you something

7 turn the computer off[turn off the
computer]

8 brush my teeth

9 go out

Track 53

p.10

Master words & chunks!

(순서 상관없음)

having fun, 재미있게 놀고 있는

eating dinner, 저녁을 먹고 있는

going to school, 학교에 가고 있는

listening to you, 네 말을 듣고 있는

playing a game, 게임을 하고 있는

sitting behind you, 네 뒤에 앉아 있는

talking on the phone, 전화 통화를 하고
있는

thinking about something, 무언가를 생
각하고 있는

looking for something, 무언가를 찾고 있는

Master sentences!

I'm

1 thinking about something

2 listening to you

3 sitting behind you

4 eating dinner

5 playing a game

6 talking on the phone

7 looking for something

8 going to school

9 having fun

Track 54

p.12

Master words & chunks!

(순서 상관없음)

eating lunch, 점심을 먹고 있는

wearing a blue shirt, 파란색 셔츠를 입고
있는

making loud noises, 시끄러운 소리를 내
고 있는

standing by the door, 문 옆에 서 있는

sitting by the window, 창가에 앉아 있는

looking in the mirror, 거울을 보고 있는

coming out of the classroom, 교실 밖
으로 나오고 있는

talking about her new class, 그녀의 새
로운 반에 대해 말하고 있는

whispering to her friend, 그녀의 친구에
게 귓속말하고 있는

Master sentences!

He's

1 coming out of the classroom

2 eating lunch

3 sitting by the window

4 making loud noises

She's

5 looking in the mirror

6 whispering to her friend

7 wearing a blue shirt

8 talking about her new class

9 standing by the door

Track 55
p.14

Master words & chunks!

(순서 상관없음)

going home, 집에 가고 있는
feeling okay, 기분이 괜찮은
having fun, 재미있게 놀고 있는
being honest, 솔직하게 하고 있는
kidding me, 나에게 농담하고 있는
coming or not, 오고 있는지 아닌지
waiting for someone, 누군가를 기다리고 있는
studying for the test, 시험공부를 하고 있는
looking for something, 무언가를 찾고 있는

Master sentences!

> Are you

1 studying for the test
2 looking for something
3 feeling okay
4 being honest
5 going home
6 coming or not
7 having fun
8 waiting for someone
9 kidding me

Track 56
p.16

Master words & chunks!

(순서 상관없음)

playing outside, 밖에서 놀고 있는
thinking about it, 그것에 대해 생각하고 있는
helping my mom, 엄마를 도와드리고 있는
taking a shower, 샤워를 하고 있는
looking for you, 너를 찾고 있는
talking to my friend, 내 친구와 이야기하고 있는
sitting in a classroom, 교실 안에 앉아 있는
sleeping on the couch, 소파에서 자고 있는
getting ready to leave, 떠날 준비를 하고 있는

Master sentences!

> I was

1 thinking about it
2 getting ready to leave
3 playing outside
4 helping my mom
5 sitting in a classroom
6 looking for you
7 taking a shower
8 sleeping on the couch
9 talking to my friend

Track 57
p.18

Master words & chunks!

(정답 순서대로)

your idea
the answer
the plan
that noise
your favorite TV show
the matter
날짜
your name
점심 메뉴

Master sentences!

> What's

1 the answer
2 the lunch menu
3 the matter
4 your favorite TV show
5 your name
6 your idea
7 the date
8 the plan
9 that noise

Track 58
p.20

Master words & chunks!

(순서 상관없음)

need, 필요하다
think, 생각하다
mean, 의미하다
do for fun, 재미를 위해 ~을 하다
like about her, 그녀의 ~을 좋아하다
have in your hand, 너의 손 안에 가지고 있다
hate the most, 가장 싫어하다
want to eat, 먹고 싶다
feel like doing, ~을 하고 싶어 하다

Master sentences!

What do you

1 do for fun
2 hate the most
3 think
4 feel like doing
5 need
6 mean
7 like about her
8 want to eat
9 have in your hand

Track 59

p.22

Master words & chunks!

(정답 순서대로)
talking about
~을 먹고 있는
waiting for
~을 하고 있는
looking at
thinking about
laughing at
planning to do
~을 읽고 있는

Master sentences!

What are you

1 looking at
2 eating
3 laughing at
4 doing
5 reading
6 waiting for

7 talking about
8 planning to do
9 thinking about

Track 60

p.24

Master words & chunks!

(정답 순서대로)
your best friend
your class president
your homeroom teacher
네 옆에 있는 남자아이
that boy over there
that girl with long hair
this girl in the picture
빨간 티셔츠를 입은 남자아이

Master sentences!

Who is

1 the boy next to you
2 this girl in the picture
3 your class president
4 your best friend
5 your homeroom teacher
6 the boy in the red T-shirt
7 that boy over there
8 that girl with long hair

Track 61

p.26

Master words & chunks!

(순서 상관없음)
say that, 그것을 말하다
like the singer, 그 가수를 좋아하다
hate him, 그를 싫어하다
think so, 그렇게 생각하다
look so sad, 매우 슬퍼 보이다
get upset, 속이 상하다
want to have it, 그것을 가지고 싶어 하다
keep looking in the mirror, 거울을 계속 들여다보다
keep bothering me, 나를 계속 귀찮게 하다

Master sentences!

Why do you

1 hate him
2 look so sad
3 want to have it
4 say that
5 like the singer
6 get upset
7 keep bothering me
8 think so
9 keep looking in the mirror

Track 62

p.28

Master words & chunks!

(순서 상관없음)

go outside, 밖으로 나가다
go together, 같이 가다
share, 같이 쓰다
ride bikes, 자전거를 타다
watch a movie, 영화를 보다
ask our teacher, 선생님께 여쭤보다
have some ice cream, 아이스크림을 먹다
switch seats, 자리를 바꾸다
meet, 만나다

Master sentences!

Why don't we

1 go together
2 go outside
3 share
4 watch a movie
5 meet
6 ride bikes
7 switch seats
8 ask our teacher
9 have some ice cream

Track 63

p.30

Master words & chunks!

(정답 순서대로)

your house
my backpack
the bathroom
my green T-shirt
your school
그 포도 주스
the bus stop
my umbrella
엄마

Master sentences!

Where is

1 your house
2 my green T-shirt
3 the bathroom
4 the bus stop
5 your school
6 that grape juice
7 my umbrella
8 Mom
9 my backpack

Track 64

p.32

Master words & chunks!

(순서 상관없음)

see me, 나를 보다
buy it, 그것을 사다
find it, 그것을 찾다
put the ball, 공을 놓다
learn Taekwondo, 태권도를 배우다
hear that, 그것을 듣다
go for vacation, 휴가를 가다
take this picture, 이 사진을 찍다
lose your umbrella, 너의 우산을 잃어버리다

Master sentences!

Where did you

1 buy it
2 take this picture
3 put the ball
4 go for vacation
5 see me
6 hear that

7 find it
8 lose your umbrella
9 learn Taekwondo

Track 65
p.34

Master words & Chunks!

(순서 상관없음)

feel, 느끼다
do that, 그것을 하다
get there, 그곳에 가다, 그곳에 도착하다
play this game, 이 게임을 하다
make new friends, 새로운 친구들을 사귀다
turn this on[turn on this], 이것을 켜다
get such good grades, 그렇게 좋은 성적을 받다
spend your free time, 너의 자유 시간을 보내다
spend your allowance, 너의 용돈을 쓰다

Master sentences!

> **How do you**

1 spend your free time
2 spend your allowance
3 do that
4 play this game
5 feel
6 make new friends
7 get there
8 get such good grades
9 turn this on[turn on this]

Track 66
p.36

Master words & Chunks!

(순서 상관없음)

come, 오다
start, 시작하다
be ready, 준비되다
see her, 그녀를 만나다
tell her, 그녀에게 말하다
be free, 시간이 나다
take a break, 잠시 쉬다

leave, 떠나다, 출발하다
bring it back, 그것을 돌려주다

Master sentences!

> **When are you going to**

1 come
2 see her
3 tell her
4 leave
5 be ready
6 be free
7 bring it back
8 start
9 take a break

Track 67
p.38

Master words & Chunks!

(정답 순서대로)

훌륭한 생각
a poor cat
a cool gift
놀라운 일
a mess
굉장한 이야기
실망스러운 것[사람]
a silly thing to say

Master sentences!

> **What**

1 a cool gift
2 an amazing story
3 a great idea
4 a poor cat
5 a silly thing to say
6 a mess
7 a surprise
8 a disappointment

Track 68
p.40

Master words & Chunks!

(순서 상관없음)

hurry up, 서두르다
be careful, 조심하다
look at this, 이것을 보다
wait a minute, 잠깐 기다리다
do it this way, 그것을 이렇게 하다
come with me, 나와 함께 가다
give it back to me, 나에게 그것을 돌려주다
leave me alone, 나를 혼자 내버려 두다
keep going, 계속하다, 계속 가다

Master sentences!

1 Be careful
2 Do it this way
3 Hurry up
4 Leave me alone
5 Look at this
6 Give it back to me
7 Wait a minute
8 Come with me
9 Keep going

Track 69
p.42

Master words & chunks!

(순서 상관없음)
worry, 걱정하다
tell anybody, 누군가에게 말하다
call me that, 나를 그렇게 부르다
bother me, 나를 귀찮게 하다
be scared, 무서워하다
cut in line, 새치기하다
make me angry, 나를 화나게 하다
make fun of me, 나를 놀리다
forget to bring it back, 그것을 돌려주는 것을 잊어버리다

Master sentences!

Don't

1 call me that
2 cut in line
3 make me angry
4 worry
5 tell anybody
6 forget to bring it back

7 be scared
8 bother me
9 make fun of me

Track 70
p.44

Master words & chunks!

(순서 상관없음)
go outside, 밖으로 나가다
play a game, 게임하다
meet at five, 다섯 시에 만나다
take a break, 잠시 쉬다
do it quickly, 그것을 빨리하다
have lunch together, 점심을 함께 먹다
get started, 시작하다
get together, 만나다, 모이다
go back to the classroom, 교실로 돌아가다

Master sentences!

Let's

1 do it quickly
2 take a break
3 meet at five
4 have lunch together
5 go outside
6 go back to the classroom
7 get started
8 play a game
9 get together

memo ✍

memo ✎

memo ✎